# Nomad of the Spirit

Bernardin Schellenberger

# NOMAD
# OF THE SPIRIT

*Reflections of a Young Monastic*

TRANSLATED FROM GERMAN BY
JOACHIM NEUGROSCHEL

FOREWORD BY
BASIL PENNINGTON

CROSSROAD · NEW YORK

1981
The Crossroad Publishing Company
575 Lexington Avenue, New York, NY 10022

Originally published as *Ein anderes Leben*
© 1980 Verlag Herder Freiburg im Breisgau
English translation copyright © 1981 by
The Crossroad Publishing Company

Printed in the United States of America

Library of Congress Cataloging in Publication Data

Schellenberger, Bernardin, 1944–
    Nomad of the spirit.

    Translation of: Ein anderes Leben.
    1. Monastic and religious life. 2. Schellenberger,
Bernardin, 1944–  . I. Title.
BX2435.S3613 1981      271′.125′024      81–5363
ISBN 0–8245–0075–X                       AACR2

# Contents

# Foreword

One of the first articles I published was entitled, "Let Us All Be Pilgrims." It was in 1950, a Holy Year when there was a real pilgrimage fever. As I wrote the article I was thinking primarily of the pious travel to shrines that had held my imagination ever since I first read Chaucer. Soon after publishing the article I took off on a pilgrimage of my own, a pilgrimage which in the Providence of God led into the life long pilgrimage of monasticism.

One of the delights of the pilgrim's way, as Chaucer so well brought out, is the coming together with others on the journey and sharing tales. There are some who lift up your heart and liven your gait as the vision of the goal shines through their eyes. There are others who are content to amble pleasantly along and notice the joys of the route. And there are those who see the dark side of things. They know the dangers of the way and show you the blisters on their heels. They call you to lighten your pack and stiffen your courage.

Bernardin Schellenberger is one of these latter. It is a joy to encounter this fellow monastic from another land, an ardent young man intent upon the same journey and candidly sharing some of the fruit of his sixteen years of journeying in a Cistercian cloister. Yet I find a certain incompleteness in the scene he depicts. I would like to see all more irradiated by the Taboric Light which is so at the heart of the monastic experience. The Vision on the Mountain needs ever to call forth our all too fragile hope. The inner reality, that we are indeed already risen in the Risen Christ, keeps our hearts beating and vitalizes our wearying limbs.

But as disconcerting as it may be, we—especially we affluent Westerners—need to be more in touch with the darker side of reality that Father Bernardin so emphasizes. With our heads too much in the clouds or clomping along too comfortably in well caparisoned vehicles, we can totally miss the Samaritan in the ditch, the starving Somali limping along the side, the sister from El Salvador who must take her unfaltering steps dragging her leg irons. We don't see, or we don't want to see, lest we be impelled to stop and come down to bind up wounds, share provisions, and loosen chains. Indeed we do not need to go so far afield, but can look to our own slums and indeed to our own families and parishes to find brothers and sisters starving, if not for food, then for human respect and decency, affirmation, love, and a word of faith.

Bernardin is a monk and speaks as a monk; he speaks first and above all to monks. And it is we, the comfortable monks of America, who most need to hear him. But every Christian, every person is on this pilgrimage. The challenge of world solidarity, universal compassion, risen life, and divine transcendence is addressed to all of us. As Father very honestly and openly shares his own struggles to break loose into the freedom of honest living, he encourages us to shake off the shackles of our false securities and

narrow concerns so that we can enter into the full possession of our being as true sons and daughters, one with the
very Son of God. May we have the courage not only to
hear this monk through but actually to let him challenge
our lives and call forth in us a liberating response.

*M. Basil Pennington O.C.S.O.*

# Introduction

The jacket of this book depicts two tree trunks looming uselessly in the landscape. Their decorative quality is a matter of taste. Hardly any life can be left in them; they are no good for construction purposes; their fuel value must be low. At best, one might build a cross out of them. And yet they make a statement, these two monuments of suffered life, these two lonesome beings, which silently converge at some point far beyond the range of this picture.

According to an old German saying, no tree has ever grown into the heavens. Today we painfully feel the truth of these words. We have succeeded in flying to the moon and to Mars, yet the greater our knowledge becomes, the farther away heaven moves from us.

Oddly enough, these feelings are shared by many people who make a sincere effort to seek God loyally and patiently. Despite all methods and technologies, He seems to conceal Himself more and more.

Anyone who honestly tries to sink his roots into the earth alongside the river of faith will not immediately see the truth in the first psalm's tantalizing promise: "He is like a tree . . . that yields its fruit in its season, and its leaf does not wither. In all that he does, he prospers."

No, the seeker of God does not flourish like the palm tree, nor does he grow like a cedar of Lebanon (Psalm 92). Nor does the Church as a whole offer the image of a plantation of green olive trees in the House of their God (Psalm 52). We do not know why this is so or why this must be so. We know only *that* faith has meaning because it is linked essentially with the fate of Jesus Christ, whose violently aborted life and broken body reveal to us a completely different God and a completely different life.

A monk's life, as I experience it, is rooted in this ground of Christian existence. I therefore hope that this book may help a few brothers and sisters to see their lives and their destinies in the light of faith and to prevail, so that we may all become signposts in the landscape of our era and have something to say to one another, and so that a new life may arise, or simply that we will have the patience to wait for the fire from heaven, which can transform even the most parched tree.

*Bernardin Schellenberger*

# A Completely Different Life

## The Romantic Misunderstanding

From the seventeenth to the early nineteenth century, courtly parks and grounds contained not only a preserve for rare and exotic animals, but also a picturesque hermitage that included, if possible, a real hermit. These ornamental hermits were the forerunners of our modern garden dwarves. Being an ornamental hermit was an actual profession. When a job opened up, the employer might even run a newspaper advertisement for a new man. In one such eighteenth-century want ad, Charles Hamilton stipulated the following conditions for the job at the hermitage in the park of Pain's Hill, Surrey:

> The Hermit must remain in the Hermitage for at least seven years. He shall be provided with a Bible, optical Glasses, a Footmat, a Prayer-Stool, an Hour-Glass, and with Water and Food from the House. He is to wear a Camelot Robe and must never, under any Circumstances, cut his Hair, his Beard, or his Nails, nor

shall he leave the estate of Mr. Hamilton or speak with
his Servants.

After seven years of living as an anchorite, this hermit
was to receive seven hundred pounds. But the hermit who
was eventually hired for the Pain's Hill hermitage had to
be fired just three weeks later because he had sneaked into
a tavern. Mr. Hamilton evidently set great store by an
"authentic" hermit existence.

If no living hermit were to be found, then a life-sized
hermit figure could fit the bill. In 1793, the German novelist Jean Paul Richter described the Bayreuth Hermitage:

> Nine mossy Fathoms of Wood. . . . The Fathoms
> surrounded a Hermitage, which—because not a Soul at
> Court had the Makings of a live Hermit—was entrust-
> ed to a wooden one, who perched within, silently and
> sensibly, meditating and reflecting as much as is possi-
> ble for such a Man. The Anchorite had been provided
> with a few ascetic Tomes, which fitted him properly,
> admonishing him to mortify his Flesh . . .

Whenever the ladies and gentlemen of the court
strolled through the park, they would visit this hermitage
in order to feel a romantic, holy shiver run up and down
their spines. In Bayreuth, at the beginning of the eigh-
teenth century, Margrave Georg Wilhelm, his spouse Wil-
helmina (the sister of the enlightened Frederick the
Great), and his court sometimes played at being hermits.
The entire group would drape themselves in picturesque
cowls and lodge in the small tufa caves that were scattered
in the forest and connected to the main building by an
irregularly winding path. A tiny bell would summon the
lords and ladies to prayers.

The significance of an institution such as the hermitage

is explained by C. C. L. Hirschfeld in his comprehensive work *Theorie der Gartenkunst* ([Theory of the Art of Gardening] Leipzig, 1780). The memory, aroused by the sight of such hermitages, has

> a strength for Emotions which a Heart that does not feel merely for this World likes to maintain. I do not know why we should not renew such Images, which induce gentle Feelings, so suitable for human Dignity. It is an Utterance of Virtue when the Monuments of Virtue warm our Hearts; and one comes a few Steps closer to Piety when one venerates the Place where a pious Man lies in Worship.

In the hermitage at Hagley Park, there was an inscription taken from Milton's "Il Penseroso." Hirschfeld found it so "very fitting" that he printed it verbatim:

> *And may at last my weary Age*
> *Find out the peaceful Hermitage,*
> *The hairy Gown and mossy Cell,*
> *Where I may sit and rightly spell*
> *Of every Star that Heav'n doth show,*
> *And every Herb that sips the Dew,*
> *Till old Experience do attain*
> *To something like prophetic Strain.*
> *These pleasures, Melancholy, give*
> *And I with thee will choose to live.*

This romantic, sentimental attitude—gracefully depicted by such German painters as Karl Spitzweg, Ludwig Richter, and Moritz von Schwind, and caricatured by the German humorist Wilhelm Busch—has influenced the common notion of a monk's or hermit's life down to the present. Even today, the back view of a monk wearing a huge hood and gazing mournfully into a vast landscape or across a still làke or reading an ancient tome, is standard fare in the brochures and picture books in which we present our way of life to the general public. There is no dearth of people who express their gratitude and esteem that we monks "still" exist. They say that they sincerely envy us for living a more quiet, more intense, more fulfilled life—the kind of life that they yearn for, too.

Thus, we monks continue to feed this misunderstanding of monastic life à la ornamental hermit. We embody and confirm certain wishes, dreams, yearnings, and illusions that are part of many people—dreams and yearnings, to be sure, that these people would never seriously follow in shaping their own lives. For they correctly sense that this kind of life is not really livable; that it can be realized, at best, by stuffed or painted hermits.

### An Ideal Far from Practical Daily Experience

In the eyes of earnest, sober people and Christians, such a monastic life is a curiosity, not truly credible or forcefully expressive. It is surely no coincidence that when a film about a Carthusian monastery in Italy was telecast in Germany some years ago, it was shown as part of a series entitled "Preserves and Sanctuaries"!

If this were merely the result of a misinterpretation by outsiders, a misreading and misunderstanding by the poorly informed, then we could regard it as unavoidable. Far more serious is our own continued support of such notions; we, too, have to struggle with them. And often, we waste too much energy enduring the wide gap between an illusory ideal and the reality we experience day after day. How many conflicts have arisen, how many crises of calling have erupted, how many callings have foundered in disillusion because monks and nuns were forced to realize after their novitiates that they had swiftly become anything but silent, meditative people living in sacred leisure, and that their communities were not exactly bodies of harmonious, peaceful togetherness? Yet this was what they were supposed to be; this was how they were described in countless texts on the monastic tradition. And this is expected of them in the Church even today.

Pope Paul VI, for example, said in his sermon of October 24, 1964, at Monte Cassino:

> Yes indeed, the Church and the world need to have St. Benedict reemerge in the community of the Church and Society, seclude himself in a preserve of isolation and silence, and let the enchanting sound of his deep and peaceful prayer go forth. From there, let him beguile us, as it were, and summon us into his cloistered sanctuary in order to show us the model of a workshop of "Divine Service," a small ideal society, where, at last, love prevails, obedience, innocence, as well as freedom from all things and the skill to use it properly, the precedence of the spirit, peace—in a word: the Gospel.

Any insider will respond to such a description with sadness, resignation, sarcasm, or indifference—depending on his temperament. The image and ideal are somehow "correct," of course. And yet they are not correct; they are a bit remote from the practical, everyday experience of monastic life. Naturally, our ideal and our goal are the full realization of the Gospel, with all the fruits of love, of the peace and joy that are promised for love. This is not the problem. The problem is that we feel pressured (or we pressure ourselves) to experience this ideal as if it had been attained already, here and now, and to embody it and therefore to keep up this pretense for ourselves and others. Rather than giving us courage and drive, this paralyzes us.

In other words, we lack a realistic concept of the monk as he could actually exist here and now—a model with which we can truly identify. And because this concept is missing, we have the typical reactions casued by an unrealistic ideal. On the one hand, we have the "incorrigibles," who remain true to this ideal and sadly hail it from afar with guilt feelings, with disappointment or dissatisfaction about their actual situations. On the other hand, we have the "pragmatists," who are usually in the majority. They have left behind the questions of an ideal and a concept of life as childish dilemmas for novice–masters and novices and for people who don't have enough to do. The satisfying, practical task lies inside or outside the monastery. These two reactions to an unrealistic ideal are brought into balance when, in a half–hearted and almost schizoid urge, one performs a considerable quota of prayers and an even more suitable quota of work, and one tells people that the meaning and justification of this way of life can be grasped only in faith.

This attitude seems to keep all further questions and objections at bay. Monks devote a considerable portion of each day to prayers, as anyone can easily see. Either you believe in the meaning and fruitfulness of vicarious prayer, which justifies monastic life, or you do not. If you do not, then you understand nothing about monastic life— or, at most, you understand only its "useful" sidelines.

*Prayer and Life with No True*
*Relationship to Reality*

The highly questionable aspect of this argument is that it uncritically presumes an almost craftlike notion of prayer, categorizing it as one of the many jobs within the Church. Some people tend the sick, others missionize, still others take care of the administrative work in the dioceses and benefices, while monks simply pray and praise God. Liturgical prayer is their specific handicraft, as it were.

Until the Second Vatican Council, this was expressed with particular clarity: the Church pressed a very old and venerable, precisely detailed, immutable Latin *officium* into the hands of monks. Their job was to perform, recite, celebrate this Divine Office every single day on behalf of the Church. The very vocabulary betrays an understanding of prayer that could be labeled materialistic. Naturally, the breviary and the choral prayer have never—or have very seldom—been construed in a totally external, technical sense. Monks were always urged to appropriate subjectively and perform spiritually what they were singing and praying. Nonetheless, there was a tendency to understand prayer in an objective sense and to separate it in practice from the essential questions of lifestyle, asceticism, and personal, individual experience. Yet these issues are actually of cardinal significance to prayer. True praying means focusing on God with one's entire existence. Tell me how you live and I'll tell you how you pray.

That is why monks themselves are chiefly occupied with praying in this externalized sense, and with working, while writers who have long since lost any contact with the experience of Christian monks are now the only ones who convincingly treat the basic questions of monastic life: for instance, loneliness, boredom, surfeit; confronta-

tion with suffering and death; dealing with our present–
day civilization; the meaning of human existence; the possibilities and tensions of human contact. A novelist and
playwright such as the Austrian Peter Handke, with his
secularized monastic experiences and questions, will have
a hard time finding a Christian monk to talk to on his own
level. Monks appear to have little time or sympathy for
mysticism, spirituality, and meditation (although, fortu-
nately, a few Jesuits have specialized in them). Monks are
far too busy keeping their monastic institutions going for
such study.

Thirty years ago, on December 20, 1949, Thomas Merton noted in his diary:

> Rilke's notebooks have so much power in them that
> they make me wonder why no one writes like that in
> monasteries. Not that there have not been better books
> written in monasteries, and books more serene. But
> monks do not seem to be able to write so well—and it
> is as if our professional spirituality sometimes veiled
> our contact with the naked realities inside us. It is a
> common failing of monks to lose themselves in a collec-
> tive, professional personality—to let themselves be cast
> in a mold. Yet this mold does not seem to do away with
> what is useless or even unpleasant about some per-
> sonalities. We cling to our eccentricities and our selfish-
> ness, but we do so in a way that is no longer interesting
> because it is after all mechanical and vulgar.
> *The Sign of Jonas* [New York: Harcourt Brace, 1953],
> p. 251)

## Drilling Down to the Source

My earlier comments and the following thoughts are not
meant to spoil anyone's enjoyment of Gregorian chant,

traditional liturgy, and many old forms and customs—especially since I enjoy them myself and would consider it foolish to toss them all away without finding a truly better and more substantial replacement. Nor do I wish to deprive anyone of the title of "monk" by defining it too sharply or narrowly. A man deserves this title if he commits his energy to spiritual welfare, teaching, and works of love rather than remaining inside a monastery's walls, doing something trivial, and imagining that this alone makes for the contemplative life. Nor do I wish to dishearten anyone who is spending his entire life behind cloistered walls and not doing anything demonstrable because, strangely enough, this appears to be his calling.

My goal is to try to drill down to the flowing lava of our monastic—nay, Christian, human—vocation; the lava from which our form of life once congealed and from which it must always renew its strength and inspiration; the lava from which it is always liquefied or relativized anew, so that our individual actions might not be all that important; the lava that establishes a living, essential contact with Jesus Christ and his fate and that enables us to find a true and earnest rapport with all people who are mentally alert and filled with today's restless seeking, no matter how they view the world, no matter what they believe in.

What I await from this hot, flowing source is a new vitality as well as practical consequences for our concrete life. I do not know whether I can carry out this vast program, but in any event, I wish to describe some of the things I have stumbled upon in my drilling, some of the things that allow me to live and that fortify me. I would be satisfied if I could help a few others see a bit more clearly and assert their lives and their strange and fascinating vocations with new strength.

*The Prophet in the "Hole" Between the*
*Present and the Future*

The Book of Ezekiel relates how the prophet was called
upon by God to perform a sign, a token:

> The word of the Lord came to me: "Son of man, you
> dwell in the midst of a rebellious house, who have eyes
> to see, but see not, who have ears to hear, but hear not;
> for they are a rebellious house. Therefore, son of man,
> prepare yourself an exile's baggage, and go into exile
> by day in their sight; you shall go like an exile from your
> place to another place in their sight. Perhaps they will
> understand, though they are a rebellious house. You
> shall bring out your baggage by day in their sight, as
> baggage for exile; and you shall go forth yourself at
> evening in their sight, as men do who must go into
> exile. Dig through the wall in their sight, and go out
> through it. In their sight you shall lift the baggage upon
> your shoulder, and carry it out in the dark; you shall
> cover your face, that you may not see the land; for I
> have made you a sign for the house of Israel."
>
> (Ezek. 1:6)

This "betokening" of Ezekiel for Israel graphically expresses an essential aspect of the monastic calling. Monks
are summoned to remind their brothers and sisters that
they are *in* the world, but not *of* this world (cf. John
17:14f.); that even if—or precisely—*when* the Church can
live unchallenged and develop its activities and its organi-
zation, we Christians live "in exile," we are pilgrims and
strangers, on the road to perfection. We have an inkling
that perfection is right here on earth, although far away,
and that it can and should come true right here, yet will
become a reality only in the kingdom of God.

Monks are like people who are driven into the night

from the finest, cheeriest festal hall because they suddenly feel that, while this banquet is merely a foreboding, a likeness, indeed a sacrament of what is to come, the future will be altogether different from the extension and profundity of all earthly joy and fulfillment. Even under the most ideal circumstances, this worldly time always has a degree of incongruence between the earthly and the heavenly kingdom and a rather vast measure of blindness, deafness, and rebellion of the world toward God. God loves the world so much that He sent His own Son into it (John 3:16). But the world is tragically incapable of receiving Him; it opposes Him and hates Him (cf. John 1:10f, 7:7, 14:17, 15:18, etc.). And this "world," this bastion of resistance to God, lies deep in the marrow of the Church itself and deep in the heart of every Christian, so that even "a righteous man falls seven times" (Prov. 24:16), that is, he shuts himself off from God and he goes his own way.

Anyone who has studied even a bit of the history of the "Christian" West will realize easily enough how massively the "world" keeps breaking into even the inner space of Christian culture. Hence, we can be assailed by doubts whether such an inner space is at all worth aspiring to. In situations of exile, the Church normally seems far more credible and consistent.

To put it perhaps a bit too subtly and paradoxically: Monachism exists because sin exists; and monachism will exist as long as sin exists. In other words, monastic life is a provisional institution that is meant to terminate itself— a form of life that would be and will be unnecessary when there is no more sin and no more incongruity between the earthly and the heavenly kingdom. If Israel were not a rebellious people, blind and deaf toward its God, the prophet would not have to pack up and go wandering, he would not have to knock a hole in the wall and climb out through this aperture before the eyes of his people.

If the Church were simply the community of the holy, if man's earthly community were truly the City of God, then individuals would not be allowed to, would not be forced to, separate themselves from one another in order to go outside their gates and make their sacrifices to God "in the desert" (cf. Exod. 4:3; Heb. 13:13f.). For Christians, isolation is never an ideal or an ultimate goal. It is always a necessary evil, a temporary destiny, a calling to participate in the isolation of Christ, as a transitional stage toward a goal: the community of the holy in the bosom of the Trinity and the inconceivable overmeasure of communication and communion of the redeemed.

But so long as this is not yet attained and not yet true, then the prophet has his calling. He must visibly make us aware of the exile situation, the unsuitability, the condition of not yet having arrived. Likewise, the Church's calling is to try and work with all people of goodwill in order to prepare the way for the kingdom of God, to maintain a mistrust against any sort of cheap optimism, to yearn for the City that cannot be built from the earth to heaven, but which must come down from heaven (cf. Apoc. 21:2) as a free gift and a pure grace.*

---

*My fellow friar Georg remarked when reading this passage: "Monasticism is a provisional condition that cancels itself out when the kingdom of God is truly and completely here. That is correct. This 'provisional state' is supposed to teach us to practice a basic attitude, and won't this basic attitude remain even then—the attitude of always starting out again, always 'further and further,' 'more and more'? For, what is perfection? Is it the kingdom of God completely arrived, the 'possession of God' for blissful contemplation and love? Perhaps we imagine it too literally in terms of the model of 'owning' and 'having': perfection as perfect knowledge, cognition, ownership, possession, etc.—a rather static and boring notion, and therefore a false one. Perfection means coming close to the secret of God, His incomprehensibility. We 'possess' Him fully by

*The Experience of the Prophet as the*
*Basic Experience of Our Time*

Is this not precisely the truth that we keep running up against nowadays on a massive scale? Is this not *the* experience that keeps urging itself upon us moderns more and more strongly, more and more ruthlessly; after a phase of naive progressivism, when we believed that our world and we ourselves were evolving linearly toward a better and better society, toward greater and greater justice, harmony, peace, prosperity, and happiness? Do people not feel more than ever—especially in our affluent countries—the incongruence between the earthly and the heavenly kingdom?

More precisely, what is the reason for their despair, their overabundance of facts, their aggression toward the existing, even rather well–functioning political and economic systems? Is it not because they have weighed them and found them wanting? They feel hopelessly washed up on the strand of this world, and they are, perhaps deliberately, blind to a new horizon, because, as it is written in the Book of Ezekiel: "They have eyes to see and do not see / And ears to hear and do not hear." They see no way out of the kingdom of earth, and do not wish to believe any longer in a kingdom of heaven.

It is bizarre and unsettling to observe that, in the light

---

allowing ourselves into Him more and more, further and further, while forgoing all 'ownership.' Hence, is the present 'provisional state' all that remote from 'perfection'? This does not strike me as being at all the case in the basic attitude. If our aim is to experience God, what is the perfection of this experience? Not the comprehensive knowledge, the comprehensive cognition, but the openness to newer and newer experiences; never being established once and for all; God as eternal spring, eternal youth, an eternal new morning. . . ."

of this situation, there are "betokenings" today like that of Ezekiel. However, the people responsible for them have normally drifted away from the Church and religion; and there is no longer any relationship between their sense of life and the tidings of the Church.

At the 1977 documenta exhibit in Kassel, a man named Stuart Brisley vegetated in a hole in the ground for two weeks, demonstrating "survival" until he lost his awareness of time. He lives in Hamburg in a locked room furnished only with a flat-roofed wooden shelter and a chair. The floor is strewn with wet sand, the wallpaper and windows are smeared with wet sand. Through cracks in two doors, one may watch Brisley in blue jeans and a green jacket, ritually sitting on the chair, mechanically looking about, marching in a rectangle, and sometimes enigmatically staring at his audience through sunglasses also smeared with wet sand. He calls this performance "Face to Face."

In New York's Squat Theater, performers in a conventional living room unexpectedly hear a radio message from the deceased German terrorist Ulrike Meinhof. She says that, since her death, she has been living in a tender, disciplined, and free society. She advises the inhabitants of the earth to kill themselves and make their death public. The German terrorist has become a mythical science–fiction figure, an angel of the Intergalaxy 21 Revolutionary Committee, proclaiming autoeuthanasia and the glad tidings of an ideal society in the beyond. Does this not oddly resemble the good old Christian concepts of the afterlife, and is it not, at the same time, confusing and hopelessly perverted?

A shattering experience for eyewitnesses was Jörg Vauth's fifty-five-foot-long raft carrying a "mummy." In the summer of 1978, he steered his raft from Ludwigshafen down the Rhine to Rotterdam and into the open sea, where an auto–da–fé took place. In Germany, the land of the economic miracle, Vauth wanted to remind the citizens of the old call to penitence: *"Memento mori*—Think of death!"

The times are long past when Christian monks and preachers of penitence were capable of such betokenings. But these preachers at least had a great deal more to offer than cynical and hopeless scorn for the world or morbid and ultimately despairing self-depiction. Presumably, the decorative hermits and prophets of the post–Christian era, like Mr. Hamilton's, go off to a tavern when day is done. (Their employers won't fire them, of course.) Still, they do provide us with food for thought, for they experience and depict man's fundamental situations and questions. And these are not so remote from ours or those of the prophet Ezekiel, yet we have apparently lost all connection with them. Have we perhaps lost it because we have not dealt sufficiently with the reality of our own lives?

### The Experience of the Prophet as the Basic Experience of Life in a Religious Order

For Christian monks and members of orders the fundamental concept of our vows and lifestyle involves a betokening: a pointing out, an indication of the still impending reality of the kingdom of God. To choose poverty, celibacy, and obedience is foolish and contradicts the lifestyle of the world and its ideals. Yet we have so thoroughly formalized and stylized, hence weakened, these very conditions that they no longer seem to have anything to do with man's true poverty, true isolation, and true lack of freedom today. Originally, the vows were supposed to mean that, by vocation and out of love for Christ, we voluntarily choose a kind of life into which many people are thrust involuntarily, and that we live as models, showing how a lover—or, to phrase it more cautiously, someone directed toward love—can live meaningfully in the most intense way, thereby overcoming this situation from within.

The way we live and the spirit we live in ought to have something to say to the poor, the lonesome, the unfree. Indeed, they ought to have a redeeming and liberating effect. Of course, this effect cannot be achieved artificially. And a relevant, deeply communicative betokening cannot be constructed; it has to emerge by itself from life. For this reason, I do not want to formulate any grand desiderata and imperatives. I will limit myself to demonstrating that this fundamental condition is actually present in our conventional religious life; and that the first step would be to see this fundamental condition anew, evaluate it anew, and agree to learn from it. Little by little, we would draw practical consequences as well.

Do we not sometimes feel that we have gotten into a rut, and that we cannot go on this way—that we are far from being what we pretend to be? Are we not actually and stunningly in the very situation of the prophet who has packed his bag, pierced a hole in the wall (of safety, security, and all the clear–cut things we take for granted about a spiritual calling), and is about to climb through? Are we not like the prophet: squeezed in this hole between a shattered, crumbling tradition and an uncertain future? All our human feeling (upon a closer look, this is the feeling of the "old human being," the ponderous, comfortable romantic) balks at it. Our so-called common sense rebels against it. This is no life, being caught as we are in a hole between yesterday and tomorrow. No human being could stand it for long.

## The Burden and Cross of the Calling
## to Be a Pilgrim

How true: this is no life. But it is not *meant* to be a life—a safe, solid, certain, cozy condition. That is precisely the burden and the cross of the prophet's calling: not to lead a "normal," satisfied, quiet life, but to be a wanderer, a fugitive, a pilgrim, a stranger. And this not only in some deep, theological sense, about which one might occasionally hear a clever devotional lecture. No, indeed; it has to be in a palpable, concrete sense; one must be capable of experiencing it day after day.

The tremendous crisis of religious life during the last few decades was like a whirlwind that smashed and shattered everything that was too certain, too established, too consolidated, and too taken for granted. It made us violently aware of this dimension of our calling. In the period before the upheaval, it was easier to sing "The Lord is my Refuge and Fortress." But it was also easier to confuse things and deceive oneself that this refuge and fortress was actually not the *Lord*, but custom and convention, old and venerable rites and immemorial habits. Thus, we were put through an ordeal that was meant to smash not *us*, but these crusts as well as our past and present resistance to God. God wanted to snatch from us what we should have given him voluntarily.

The reaction to all this was understandable, but disappointing. A huge number of people in religious orders fled from this tension, this test of their endurance, to new positions of "safety," cottages and bunkers outside or inside their communities. They despaired of any meaning in cenobitic life and gave it up, entrenching themselves behind old barricades or reconciling themselves to compromises and concessions that made their salt lose its savor.

In the light of the cracks and chasms that have opened up in our concepts, notions, habits, expectations; in the light of all these futilities, seemingly wasted energies, apparently insoluble problems and conditions—we should not grow bitter or aggressive, not run away or self–pityingly cut ourselves off in frustration and resignation. Instead, all these experiences should teach us something essential about our calling; we must accept the fact that we are not really at the destination, but still en route.

Even more, in all these cracks and abysses, we should sense not the hell of hopelessness, but the shimmer of things to come, which are so great and ungraspable that they will simply have to burst, smash, destroy all our earthly systems and categories and constructions in order to widen our horizons.

## *The Experience of Taking Part in Christ's Fate*

Is this an appeal to a faith that does not coincide with experience, a demand to pretend that ill fortune is good fortune, an inhuman exhortation to live and breathe in a vacuum?

Yet there is a positive experience right *in* this situation; it is very real and better than that attainable through contrived asceticism and meditation. It is the experience of being placed in the condition of the earthly Jesus, who said that the disciple would not be better off than the master, and that a true disciple is satisfied to be as his master (Matt. 10:24f.). Do we not truly embody the fact that we find houses, brothers, and sisters in this world, albeit among persecutions and afflictions, as was prophesized for us (Mark 10:30); and that, as with Saint Paul, we are offered the ability and the experience of dying and yet living, of being sorrowful and yet always rejoicing, of being poor and yet—or precisely for that reason—making many rich (2 Cor. 6:9–10)?

## Renunciation Should Not Be Disguised

In this paradoxical situation, we are again more able to cry spontaneously and honestly: "Come, Lord Jesus!" (Rev. 22:20) And we can truly yearn for and experience this coming of the Lord as redemption, as liberation. If everything in our lives were as good, as harmonious, as satisfactory as we have always dreamt, might it not be more difficult to wish sincerely that Christ might come today instead of tomorrow and say to us: "Leave all your works and enterprises and plans and habits, for now I am here myself, and this puts an end to all those things"?

"The monastic life is not a renunciation but a choice. . . . One is choosing the friendship of Christ. . . . One is choosing everything!" says a brochure from a Benedictine monastery. This quote from the sensible Teresa of Avila is of course true on the level of faith, not necessarily on the level of everyday practical experience. Hence, it can be misleading and disheartening. It can force us into the role of people who *must* be happy because they have, after all, chosen Christ and therefore "everything." And if we do not feel happy, then we are tempted to believe that there is something wrong with our community or with ourselves. We grow confused, dissatisfied, disappointed, and we do not accept this experience of unfulfillment positively, as a part of our life and our experience.

## Renunciation as a Radical Way
## of Keeping Oneself Open

How would it be if we said to ourselves somewhat less idealistically, but more realistically, "Monastic life does mean renouncing something. And one feels this renunciation." Property, personal freedom, personal completion through marriage—these are basic values, fundamental human rights, normal aspects of human growth. Anyone forgoing such basic rights will sometimes feel their lack quite distinctly. A wound emerges, a vacuum; something remains unfulfilled. And this empty space is not promptly and effortless filled, let alone overfilled, by Christ's love and by spiritual experience.

Certainly, the person who loves God will gladly accept this burden. He may feel like Jacob, who had to serve Laban for twice seven years until he received Laban's beautiful daughter Rachel as his wife: "And they seemed to him but a few days because of the love he had for her" (Gen. 29:20). But no amount of love can conceal the fact that true fulfillment is still missing; that everyday life means "servitude." Few are the hours when one ambles through a flowery meadow, strumming a guitar and leading a group of merry children (one convent regularly uses such a photo to recruit new sisters). Let us therefore say in all honesty that a monk's life, a life in a religious order, cannot offer you a warm nest. All it can give you is a nomad's tent, which at times may be pretty cold and drafty.

Dealing with God is not without its dangers. One may have to wage struggles in the dark, from which, as with Jacob, one may reel forth blessed but also groggy and limping. Let us be honest with ourselves and with others: monastic life is not a "normal" life. Strictly speaking, it is an "impossible" life—an open, an exposed, an unfulfilled life—because it is geared to Him who is to come. And let us not soften this claim by trivializing it; by making poverty, obedience, solitude too comfortable; by toning down their demands with all the fine excuses and arguments that the inventive mind of our "old human being" (the comfortable romantic) can so swiftly come up with.

Isn't it true that, for many so–called "worldly Christians," social dependencies, professional necessities, and familial obligations are far more powerful and more concrete in the obedience and self-denial they require than the obligations accepted reluctantly and self-pityingly by many of those who have publicly taken vows of obedience and self-denial? How bleak, how tedious, how banal, how insipid many lives in monastic orders have become because of the wealth of compensations and ersatz satisfactions, in themselves innocuous and innocent. And how devastatingly all deeper meaning, the whole dynamics and energy of yearning, can thereby be lulled and deadened!

Reiner Gödtel published the following poem in the *Frankfurter Allgemeine Zeitung* in May 1979: "Acting as though you didn't need orientation / Acting as though you didn't need anyone / waiting for you / happy / when you come home / Acting as though you were never depressed / Acting as though you didn't need a heart-to-heart talk / as though you didn't need any love any children any family / Acting as though on Christmas Eve / you could stand on a stool casual relaxed / and paper the walls of your empty apartment / without a secret yearning." This poem might almost be a program for celibates and cenobites in the false, inauthentic sense that it is their duty to pretend they need none of the things that are needed by a mature, healthy person with a normally developed sensibility. Of course they need these things. And of course they are deluding themselves when they do succumb to these needs in a surrogate form, openly or secretly, thereby simply erasing the tension of waiting and unfulfillment from their lives. Their calling is to live with this tension. It is a misunderstanding to believe that we are expected to be models, living an ideal—say, the ideal that "God alone suffices," or the ideal of a harmonious community— as though it had already been attained and acting as if we were the happiest people in the world.

Actually, I have never met an altogether convincing exemplar of the model monk—an ideal toward which we were trained as novices, explicitly or tacitly, and toward which our novices are still being trained: a man for whom "God alone suffices," a man who finds peace and fulfillment in prayer, meditation, and spiritual reading, and by doing some simple labor that does not require too much responsibility. In practice, everyone is constantly tempted to draw a good portion of his sense of validity, hence inner equilibrium, from devotion to "work," a task, a job—no matter how unimportant and perhaps even parochial it may seem and often is—since it is restricted to the small circle of the monastery. This is normal and should not be denied, concealed, repressed, or loaded with guilt feelings because it doesn't correspond to the ideal notion of the good and happy monk. In reality, the good monk would have to be the one who felt and recognized this need but—within the measure of the strength granted him for faith and love—kept it open and did not try to fulfill it completely.

The point is to go beyond the principles of an ideal inner state—conceived in purely mental terms—of psychological equilibrium and contentment, toward a consciously endured unfulfillment. Thus, we wish to totally and consciously live the reality of human existence, of humanness as a pilgrimage toward God; of humanness as an existence of seeking, a questioning, wrestling; of humanness as a life of suspension, of waiting for the coming of God. This presupposes a sound measure of psychological maturity. It must not be exaggerated, because it is like an advance into a no man's land, where one can starve to death if frivolity or ambition makes one venture out too far.

## Renunciation in our Time

Our renunciations ought to serve this openness. They ought to make clear that nothing but God can satisfy us, and that we want no temporary satisfactions to stave off the hunger and thirst for this one and only essential satisfaction. If we got more involved in this issue, especially as members of an affluent society, then we would presumably come far closer to the questions of the above-mentioned examples of modern "prophets," and we would have something essential to contribute.

Today, to all appearances, mankind is learning of its own accord the bitter lesson that it is not capable of autonomously creating peace, an earthly paradise, and a lasting purpose to life. And at exactly the same time, we Christians are overanxiously taking to heart the insight, no doubt correct, that we should not misuse the blessings and praises of the Sermon on the Mount in order to leave the poor in their poverty and comfort them with the promise of a better afterlife. Yet we overlook the fact that the Sermon on the Mount does indeed describe poverty, chosen voluntarily or borne out of love, as the preferred condition for experiencing God.

Down through the centuries, the saints, with irrational

passion, have always lauded drudgery, poverty, and privation because they knew they were closest to God in these states, where they actually even found Him. Have we lost this instinct of the saints? Do any of us still understand the desert father who told his brethren: "Have we not come to this place because of the drudgery? And now it gives us no more drudgery! I have arranged my cloak and I am going to a place where there is drudgery, and there I shall find peace"? Are people in the Western world sufficiently concerned that, along with their economic aid, they are also exporting their boredom, surfeit, and suicide rates to the countries of the Third World? Do they realize that it is, therefore, irresponsible to praise our own culture or nonculture as a liberating and redeeming Gospel, instead of confessing pointblank: "We're on a dead–end street ourselves and we sense very acutely that the meaning and fulfillment of human life have to be sought in an entirely different direction"?

If the worldwide campaign against material poverty does not advance along with a reawakening of the ideal of spiritual poverty, then it will lead to an infernal kind of poverty, devoid of any hope or future. These are the problems afflicting monks and religious. Such problems are found to challenge *us* to live a consistent way of life, and in fact to disquiet all Christians. Recently, Manfred Mezger wrote in the German magazine *Radius:*

> "You must live in such a way that He [Jesus] could come any day." But the people who say this don't look as if they are doing it. If one has any dealings with them, one soon notices that they don't write their essays any better, they don't bring up their children any better, they are not any more particular about telling the truth than other people. When one sees how comfortable they make their lives, one knows that Jesus

won't be coming all that soon; certainly not today; perhaps tomorrow.

### Living Between the Present-day and the Future Reality

If an unbiased vacationer happens to pass a Benedictine, Cistercian, or Carthusian monastery, he will hardly have the spontaneous impression that a few paupers of Christ have provisionally set up housekeeping until the Lord returns. Indeed, the dominant ground plan of all traditional monasteries or cloisters for the past thousand years derives from a time when monasteries were conceived as a reflection and foretaste of the heavenly city of Jerusalem, as islands of the already beginning kingdom of God. Yet the element that has always kept Christianity alive is the tension between the "already here" and the "not yet here" of the kingdom of God. There is a meaning, a necessity, a sublime grandeur in living the "already here." Yet today, without giving up this aspect or being permitted to resolve the tension, we should be admitting the aspect of the "not yet here" more powerfully and making it the formative principle of our lives. Quite simply, we are pushed into this by the situation of the world, of the Church, and of our own monastic communities.

What does this mean in practical terms? First of all, we should accept the experience of living with crises and problems positively, as an essential component of our calling. We should not regard it as an interference factor, repressing it and lamenting it as something that should not be and allowing it to paralyze us. Instead, we should, paradoxically, view it as the source of our strength and inspiration. That which chafes us keeps us awake. It constantly reminds us that our monastic life is a life on the border between that which is and that which ought to be. In a pure form, it would not be livable, for one cannot hang for long between heaven and earth without perishing. Ours is and will remain a paradoxical life. To prepare for permanence in something impermanent is an impossible task.

We can shape ourselves in such a way as never to abandon the provisional state completely and never to establish ourselves definitively. We cannot halt at one simple step "out of the world" and into a monastic order when we take our vows. Once inside the monastery, we must not see the purpose of our lives in the truck garden, the archive, the cheese factory, the convent school; in expanding this enterprise and at the same time managing a vast schedule of prayers and masses. If this happens, the monastery will merely prove that "God alone" does not suffice. It will merely offer a sample collection of the most diverse ways and means of compensating for the renunciations that issue from the vows. It will then become a closed system, running by itself and practically absorbing all energy for intramural activities, instead of inspiring the monks with an attitude of openness and preparedness for Him who is to come.

Thomas Merton once formulated two questions that could be helpful in this connection to examine toward what and for what we are living in *practice* (in *theory*, we always have high, indeed the very highest, motives). If you want to know who I am, says Merton, then ask me: What are you living for, very concretely, here and today in your everyday life? And: What do you think keeps you from living fully for what you would like to live for?

*The Experience of All Men:*
*A Borderline Existence*

Viewed more closely, these reflections on monastic life are, I think, reflections on a fundamental experience of all Christian, nay, all serious human life. Perhaps that is why they may also interest people who have no express calling to be a monk. I am grateful that I was called to monasticism, a life that I still live gladly and with tension. I have therefore formulated everything from a monk's perspective, since this is the viewpoint that I know best and most thoroughly. But my perspective is not exclusively "monkish." On the contrary, my impression is that many people live these values and experiences more intensely and more vividly than monks do. In fact, there seem to be more and more people destined to live a "borderline" existence, a life *between* the solid, clearly defined forms of a monastic community and a "worldly" vocation.

But wherever we may live—are we not all like those who have packed their things and are stuck inside the hole in the wall through which they are supposed to climb? Are we not always breaking out (or being broken out), at home in restlessness, always making attempts and wandering into solutions that are no solutions? Our faith tells us—and allows us to experience—that in this paradoxical situation, we can encounter deep and genuine joy, even if this joy may not always or may only rarely express itself in jubilation and carefree merriment.

This joy is different from the joy of Camus' Sisyphus, who seeks and apparently finds peace in submission to the absurd and in the celebration of meaninglessness. This joy lives from the mysterious oneness with Him who in His earthly days "offered up prayers and supplications, with loud cries and tears" (Heb. 5:7), and who was the first to hang between heaven and earth, not as a romantic image, but as a sign of our true situation.

# Becoming Empty for God

## Seized by the Unknown God

When a monk speaks about himself, his words are inconsistent, nay, absurd. He is nothing and he has nothing and he does nothing worth talking about. The more deeply he is seized with the mystery of his calling as the years go by, the less he can say about it. At bottom, he can speak meaningfully only about God and about Jesus Christ, who has taken everything from him and will not leave him in peace. But even talking about God is difficult, for the monk experiences more intensely when God is *not* for him than when He *is* for him. The monk can say with Job: "Behold, I go forward, but he is not there; and backward, but I cannot perceive him; on the left hand I seek him, but I cannot behold him; I turn to the right hand, but I cannot see him" (Job 23:8–9). His images and concepts and experiences of God flow away in a jumble or are violently shattered; and in the end, all he may still know is who and how God is *not*. And yet he is afflicted by this Absent One, this

Unknown One, and he cannot get away from Him, like Jeremiah, who lamented:

> *If I say, "I will not mention him,*
> *nor speak any more in his name,"*
> *there is in my heart as it were a burning fire*
> *shut up in my bones,*
> *and I am weary with holding it in,*
> *and I cannot.*

(Jer. 20:9)

In the spirituality and theology of our time, a large part is played by the insight and experience that God and the world ("world" in the sense of creation and of the reality that we find) are not poles apart. Despite the broken relationship between God and the world, God, we are told, is to be found in the depths and on the heights of the world. Hence, no rejection of the world is needed to come to God. On the contrary, man with his hunger and thirst for God, should turn his faith to the world, and there, in the heart of the world, he shall find his God.

However, a monk's basic experience is different. He does not have to leave the world, much less despise it. The world leaves *him,* just as it left Job upon the collapse of all his earthly goods and certainties, which he had administered in innocence and in fear of God.

For the monk, God is the completely Different One, the Incomprehensible, at times even the Menacing One.

The monk, to echo Saint Paul, has as yet attained nothing and is not yet complete. But everything he once viewed as a positive value, as a gain, has now become a loss for him. He is seized by Christ, and he strives to seize the new, the true, reality and fullness of his life; but he has not yet seized them (cf. Phil. 3:7, 12–13). He hangs between heaven and earth; he has not yet reached the heavens and is no longer at home on earth. He settles in a territory that is not fit for settlement. He lives among sheer contradictions. They prevent him from establishing himself and, more important, his notion of God, anywhere. Any image of God that comes from wishful thinking and projecting is to be thoroughly driven out of him. He does not find God in the lengthening and deepening of his joys, nor does he find God in the lengthening and deepening of his fears.

## *"Being Empty for God"*

The outsider and the beginner tend to see monastic life as a tranquil, shielded, perhaps even somewhat artificial existence in which one has a good deal of time and leisure for spiritual life, meditation, and prayer; they see it as a sacred milieu sanctified and dignified by Gregorian chant and a cultivated liturgy. This conception is certainly valid, in part. The novice, for whom the "joys of the world" do not appear substantial enough, will expect to find substantial, fulfilling matter and content for his life. He has a specific ideal of the "contemplative monk," who lives with and for God alone in a harmonious community of like-minded men. This ideal is confirmed by innumerable texts throughout a long tradition: being a monk means *vacare Deo*—"being free, vacationing for God"—to quote one of the most popular phrases that have come down to us.

For anyone entering monastic life, however, this overly naive conception sooner or later triggers a fundamental crisis. The novice is bound to realize that "being free" is not as easy as he imagined, and that "God" is not present as soon as he expected or in the manner that he expected. Perhaps the novice thought he would advance quickly in spiritual life once he had found enough time and space and a more favorable environment for his pious exercises, for his reading and meditating. But what he actually experiences seems like a setback: he again finds himself engulfed in tensions, in doubting all his earlier notions about monastic life. He may even feel his entire spiritual life bursting like a soap bubble. Liturgy, private prayer, meditation do not bring him the awaited fruits. On the contrary, these experiences literally dry up. And unforeseen tensions emerge everywhere. If he has a strong drift toward isolation, then he suffers from the constant demands of community life. If he enjoys company, then he will feel the burden of isolation all the more strongly. Along with these and similar tensions, he painfully notices that his brethren are dreadfully ordinary, weak, inconsistent men. Finally, he comes to realize that he *himself* is no different. He, who set out to look for God, does not find the God he expected; instead, he finds himself and his brethren with all their poverty and fallibility. Ultimately, he asks himself, perhaps in despair, whether he is in the right place; he wonders what sense all this makes or what he might have done wrong.

In reality, these feelings are normal and the only proper ones. The monk is, so to speak, systematically brought to a zero point. The phrase *vacare Deo*, "to be empty for God," reveals its ulterior meaning. The monk is to be literally hollowed out, emptied, nullified, before and for God. He must learn to let go of all his notions and expectations. Otherwise, he would quickly, imperceptibly, with a subtle, sneaky pride, take the pseudorole of a spiritually experienced man. He might fall prey to the illusion that the monastery is a kind of Christian recreational club, where the goal is to find more and more ways of keeping one's joy in God alive—and given today's rich supply of diverse thoughts, meditations, and spiritual stimuli, he will never be at a loss for material. Most likely, he would soon be producing such material himself. Or else he might assume the role of a liturgical functionary, an ecclesiastically approved leader for prayers and intercessions, who performs his "choral service" as would any government official, perhaps with a paid vacation every year, coffee breaks, and sick days. He might be led astray in this direction by a certain role expectation on the part of the others —an expectation that has, of course, grown somewhat weaker today. The contemplative monks were regarded as special workers, so to speak, in a prayer power plant that furnishes the entire Church with "grace current" through underground circuits. The contemplative monks were even likened to the Ten Righteous Men for whose sake God refrains from destroying the Sodom and Gomorrah of this world. However, these ten did not exist in Abraham's time, and they do not exist today. In any case, the monks are not among them: this is one thing they have to learn very clearly.

## Taken into the Suffering and Death of Christ

When the monk's own plans are spoiled, when God becomes more and more incomprehensible to him and more and more remote, then, one may hope, he will see the light. He will realize that his disappointment has something to do with the fate of his Lord and master, an imitation of whom he has launched into with a certain naiveté. For he could not really have divined the ultimate consequences.

I have tinged these last few sentences with a bit of sarcasm because they describe the reef on which very many

Christians founder in their spiritual development, or on which they are at least stranded (astonishing, given what they have sermonized to themselves and to others incessantly). One can never stop being amazed at how trippingly the words *imitation, carrying the cross, being crucified along with* roll over our tongues—and how we melt into self-pity when we are taken at our word. We then act as if we had not had the slightest inkling that the suffering we have so frequently spoken of meant *actual suffering* and the dying, *actual dying*. We do count on something or other being difficult along the way or hurting a little; but we expect, if not a beatific vision, then at least something of that ilk, so that nothing can get all that tragic.

The monk does not have beautiful "experiences," cultivated in leisure throughout his life as his spiritual self-confirmation. Instead, God involves him with his entire existence in a true process of dying, which signifies the completely sober and unsentimental action of being taken into the process of the fate of Jesus Christ Himself. The more the monk's fate becomes identical with Christ's fate, the less he "sees" or "finds out" or "experiences," because this identification is, in essence, not an objectifiable object that one can set down and observe.

## The Road to the Desert of Human Reality

When the monk experiences the nullification of his image of God, he learns what happened to Jesus Christ. In his end, which was failure by any human standard, He revealed the holiness of God in a seeming contradiction of that holiness. God's revelation in Jesus Christ was the total negation of all human ideas of holiness and perfection, the ideas in the minds of those, then and now, who shout under the cross: "If you are the Son of God, come down from the cross. . . . Let him come down now from the cross, and we will believe in him" (Matt. 27:40, 42).

These words echo the voice of the Tempter in the desert: "If you are the Son of God, command these stones to become loaves of bread. . . . Throw yourself down. . . . [I will give you] all the kingdoms of the world and the glory of them" (cf. Matt. 4:1–11). In the desert and on the cross, Christ confronted this abysmal, eternal temptation of man: the temptation of human, bogus divinity, the temptation to make oneself God in the image and effigy of man. However, man's road to God does not pass through the possibility that the devil offered Christ in the desert. Dostoievsky, in his "Grand Inquisitor," interprets the devil's three proposals as the temptations for miracle, mystery, and power. And these are the essential elements of self-deification, pseudoexistence, and, ultimately, self-destruction.

In contrast, Christ pointed out the only possible road to God: the radical affirmation of our humanness, with its essential poverty, sobriety, and impotence, with its mortality. That is why the Christian is baptized into the death of Christ, into His temptation, into His descent to hell, into His state of utmost sensitivity and vulnerability due to the wretchedness, helplessness, and misery of being human. The monk, who seemingly "leaves the world," is thrust into the desert by his way of life; and here, in the desert, he runs up against the consequences of his baptism, which confront him with the "world" more thoroughly and more intensely than ever. What he leaves behind is not really the "world," for he himself is the "world" through and through. He abandons certain conventions and possibilities that are normally offered, indeed thrust upon him by the "world," as a seduction to live in falseness, illusion, dispersion, and self-alienation, fleeing from the consequences of his baptism.

When Saint Anthony of Egypt went off to the desert in the fourth century, he was confronted more intensely than anyone else with the demons of the paganism of his time, and, representing the entire Church, he conquered them. When a monk is driven into the desert today, one can expect him to run up against the demons of our era. Franz Kafka once noted: "Stay at your table and listen. Don't even listen, just wait; don't even wait, just be completely quiet and alone. The world will offer itself to you to be unmasked, it cannot do otherwise, it will writhe before your eyes ecstatically." The only thing I would change in this quotation is that the isolated man is not an objective, disinterested observer of this exposure of the world; he is himself exposed and infected down to the deepest strata of his being. Thomas Merton writes: "This is precisely the monk's chief service to the world: this silence, this listening, this questioning, this humble and courageous exposure to what the world ignores about itself—both good and evil."

It would be dangerous to start out on this expedition all on one's own. Christ blazed a trail for us in the desert. Because we are in Him and are nourished by His word and sacrament, we can venture—or better, we can let ourselves be driven into the desert without despairing or losing hope and winding up in stupor or nihilism. Gradually, we can learn to endure the calling to fear, helplessness, isolation, separation in the incomprehensible God, to participation in God's remoteness in our time, to Christ's renunciation, to the participation in His redeeming death. We believe that this involvement in Christ's fate has a universal, therapeutic effect, clearing a path for the Church, and through the Church for the world, a path from enslavement by blindness and lies, from subjugation by a false, demonic (individual and collective) self-portrait and portrait of God.

## An Overly "Worldly" Image of God and Its Comfortable Consequences

The exodus of the first monks into the desert occurred at the beginning of the age of Constantine, when the Church made a compromise with the Tempter. It grabbed the property, splendor, and power that the Tempter offered it through the state. The image that believers had of God and the kingdom of God changed accordingly. The Transcendental One, with whose coming mankind had to reckon at any moment, so that it wasn't worth the trouble of establishing oneself anywhere, became a Byzantine emperor. Courtly worship and splendor, shimmering gold, riches, and power were considered the appropriate symbols of and allegories for God. In its impoverished, secularized form, this humanized concept of God is still accepted today. God is generally viewed as the endless extension of earthly prosperity and happiness in all their conceivable forms. The practical result is a Christian lifestyle with no great risk. The hope for Christ remains merely trimming for "self-realization" and for a life of fully exploited possibilities which Christians seek and utilize in accordance with the same principles as people who do not believe in Christ. If Christ had not been resurrected, then it would by no means be as tragic as Saint Paul thought (cf. 1 Cor. 15:19), for then we would have had as much and as little of life as all other people. Who can blame the growing number of our contemporaries who view the God of the Christians as dispensable? He has been degraded into a decoration, a hobby for religious–minded types, a pastime that can offer valuable possibilities for the celebration of fulfilled and fully savored humanness.

*One* purpose of monachism today could be its silent and existential questioning of this false image of God in the name of Jesus Christ. The monastic calling renounces certain comfortable habits, an acknowledged useful role in the world, a respectable career. Monks should not try to "be somebody," even in the Church. Instead of fleeing from frustrations and from their own poverty and nullity, instead of fleeing from the cross and death or else accepting these realities as inevitable only when they can no longer escape them, they should advance toward them in freedom, with and in Christ.

## The Monastery, a Place of Sober Self-knowledge

A monastery, no matter how strict, is not simply the place where one *fulfills* this demand to the bitter end. Naturally, one goes along with it on a certain superficial level by renouncing marriage, personal property, and a great deal of independence. At times, this can even be quite comfortable. However, inside the monastery, the monk again finds a certain system and a group dynamic that tends to develop rules quite analogous to those in the society "outside." Hence, certain pious role expectations and chances for power and accomplishment present themselves. By sheer external conformity or achievement, one can again create an illusory self-confirmation. Generally, monks are extremely inventive when it comes to any kind of work, action, or pious activity that serves this purpose. Nevertheless, the monastery has the advantage of making one strongly feel the altogether different standards that one *should* apply to one's conduct, but that one, inconsistently, does not apply. Many of the usual ways to compensate for one's emptiness are missing; and this absence makes one feel exposed. Anyone who flees his own calling is easier to see through, by others as well as by himself. When a monk begins to invest all his passion and energy in some blatantly meaningless activity, he soon appears ludicrous. The people around him clearly sense that something is wrong, and he senses it himself.

After sixteen years in the monastery, I can only report experiences that are mostly not very different from other people's: experiences of my own poverty, emptiness, and inconsistency. Perhaps the monastery has helped me to confront them a bit more consciously, more nakedly, more basically. I have not attained much more than the notion that my state, my development—or rather my non-development, my development into nothing, my disillusion, and my contradictory existence must have something to do with the fate of Jesus Christ. And yet this awareness, this little bit of certainty, is worth more to me than all kinds of "experiences" that I could never be sure were not just the product of my own passionate desires or fears. For as long as I greedily (however spiritual my greed) cast about for a particular experience, a particular state, I must consider that what I achieve will be the reflection, the product, of my greed—a false image of God, an idol in my own image, after my own likeness. Had I completely overcome my aggressive impatience in trying to attack, conquer, seize, and hold on to God, in trying violently to make something of myself; had I, instead, totally surrendered, totally given up, accepted my complete nullity; indeed, had I stopped even wanting anything or wanting to be anything; if this "old human being," as the New Testament calls him, the man who can only continue to bring forth the human but nothing divine, if this "old human being" had completely died—then I would enter the last and deepest poverty and loneliness that Christ entered and that, within Christ, mysteriously became God's loneliness; and then the "new human being" could come more clearly to the fore, could rise again from this death, a man who is no longer structured according to some human concept but created in the image of God, and who could thus reflect the true God.

An old desert father once described this unintentionality, this utterly profound process of making oneself free to be made rich by that which is entirely Other, a process so simple and yet so difficult that it takes a lifetime to achieve. The father said, "I will continue all my life as you see me now: a little work, a little meditation, a little prayer, and, as well as I can, I will keep myself pure of thoughts and oppose them when they come over me. But thus did the spirit of contemplation come over me, and I do not know how."

## Monks: Likenesses of the Church— *with Its Strengths and Weaknesses*

There is a widespread notion that spiritual maturity can be grasped and experienced as a linear development. This notion is false. We do not develop linearly until something "ignites," until an "illumination experience" marking the point when one sees oneself and the world in a totally new light, when one sees oneself who "is above it all" and who "has made it." On the contrary, a process of inner transformation occurs imperceptibly—"I don't know how," said the desert father—amid all the tensions, weaknesses, and inconsistencies. Often, the strains even increase rather than decrease. This persistent poverty, this paradoxical condition, is likewise a form of renunciation. Whether in their own or in other people's eyes, monks should not and cannot be an elite, a caste of completed and perfected beings in the Church. They are and always will be reflections, paradigms of the Church that is en route and not yet at the goal. An interaction exists between their condition and that of the entire Church.

In Martin Buber's *Gog and Magog,* a rabbi says, "The revealed stand on the concealed. And even in them, the revealed, that which can bear others is not their openness, but their concealment. All being that bears is concealed." All being engages in mutually concealed communication. And all of us, whether monks or so-called "secular Christians," are both revealed and concealed at once. That is why the monasteries reflect the situation of the Church; and even their imperfection is a form of solidarity with the Church and thus an integrating component of their calling. They are meant to suffer vicariously from this. Christ, too, existentially entered the state of those whom he wanted to redeem. This is why I said earlier that the image of the Perfect One who supplies grace to sinners is problematical. In fact, it is downright false.

### The "New Human Being"

The tiny spark of certainty that one stands in the fate of Jesus Christ, and thereby in Him whom one does not feel, does not experience, does not see—this spark, for which one must give everything away, absolutely everything, brings peace and freedom, that completely different peace and that completely different freedom, "not as the world gives" (cf. John 14:27). This peace and this freedom are the hallmarks of the "new human being," who can gradually emerge. I would like to say a few more things about this person.

Theophilus of Antioch once observed, "Show me your man and I'll show you your God." The "old human being of sin" clutches at a homemade image of man, and this image corresponds to a homemade, counterfeit image of God. However, the hidden God has created as his counterpart the "hidden person of the heart" (1 Pet. 3:4), his living icon. There is such an image, such a concept for every human being: his true identity in God. At first, he does not recognize it. It is disguised by his false self, the role player, the ego, which seeks itself, even on the highest strata of spiritual life and contemplation. Only when this false self-confidence, with all its ambitions, even spiritual ambitions, gives itself up and dies—only then does the true self gradually come to the fore: the likeness of God, the "new human being," the real "person" in a quality of personhood that is analogous to the personhood of the persons in the Trinity, i.e., in an ultimate, unshakeable identity with itself and also in a radical, essential relation to the others.

The novice in monastic life first takes a great step of renunciation by leaving his "worldly" life behind. But only in the rarest of cases does he also leave the "old human being" behind. This "old human being" now shifts his ambition to religious terrain and tends to regard his striving as virtuous and selfless. If he sticks to this, he will become an individual aspiring to an impossible ideal of individual holiness in a kind of spiritual solipsism. This solipsism does not take him to heaven; it takes him to the hell of hopeless isolation, to inhibition, embitterment, and hardening in certain forms of piety.

But once the spiritual plans of the "old human being"

are thwarted and he no longer desperately clings to them, then perhaps he will realize the necessity of total rebirth in the spirit of Christ. In his deepest despair his being can dissolve in Christ and he can become capable of opening up to Him, loving Him, and living out of Him. He then sees himself and the world as God does. He relates to people the way Christ does. He becomes independent of the comforts of various social "idols" and no longer rises and falls with approval from other people. He no longer seeks love, much less demands love; instead, he gives it unconditionally. He no longer asks to be loved, understood, accepted, forgiven; instead, he wishes to understand all people, love all people, forgive all people, accept others as they are, and help them to transcend themselves in love. His viewpoint is, so to speak, "outside" the world. That is why the "new human being"—like Christ—is then "useless" in this world, remaining at the edge of human society and having no practical solutions to offer.

Dostoievsky very graphically depicted such "new human beings" in his novels. The "idiot," Prince Myshkin, for instance, does not actually take part in the external course of events, or at least he does so in an altogether different way than the other characters. He is suspended in space like an icon; and the events taking place on the stage of the world can be deciphered in the icon's revealing and sanctifying light. In Dostoievsky, the "new human being" is a sign of contradiction, a man who takes part in the paradox of the Incarnation. He is the judge and the redeemer of the world, because *he* alone knows the truth of the world, and he can interpret it, *trans-late* (carry across) from God and to God. He contemplates the "Sophianic" world, the world as conceived in the beginning by the creative wisdom of God before the Fall of Man, and the "new human being's" love can bridge all the cracks caused by the Fall. He becomes the unifying, integrating force in his milieu, a center of peace and reconciliation. But he does not realize this. He has nothing, he does nothing, he possesses nothing but what he *is*. And he is profoundly convinced that he is *nothing*. Anything he does, he can do *well* and *correctly* without being concerned about how to do it. Thus, without realizing it himself, he begins to construct a "reintegrated" world, a world according to the Creator's original intention, as a participator in the divine art of shaping the world.

Yet this description almost goes too far. For, in reality, such thoroughly "new human beings" are extremely rare. We experience only pieces of them. However, such a "new human being" is contained to some extent in all of us, and we ought to let him see the light. In every monastery, in every religious community, one can find distinct traces of the shape of a "new," healed world. Over and over, here and there, we manage to live together for a while in the peace and joy of the Holy Spirit. All in all, however, we do not live in a time when "new human beings" can shape a redeemed world, build holy communities, mysterious cathedrals, and closed systems of a wisdom-imbued theology that provide a foretaste of a redeemed cosmos. Today is a time when the "new human beings" and all who look like them—I am thinking, for instance, to avoid mentioning a live person, of Pasternak's Dr. Zhivago, that man from Paradise—conflict radically with the human muddle of their social system. They can be thankful if they are not exiled to the other end of the globe, if they are permitted at least to pitch their tents at the outskirts of the city. Perhaps, some day, the time will come again when they may build. But, for now, their most perceptible participation is to suffer because of a world that is not built according to God's concepts.

Thus we return to the paradoxical situation in which the "new human being," too, remains on this earth, just like Jesus Christ. He is at once a peacemaker and a sign of contradiction. Like the "seer" in Plato's cave, he can come out, get to know true sunlight, and then return to his former companions in misfortune in order to show them the way to the light. They will declare him mad and stay with their shadows. He can consider himself lucky if they do not finally kill him so as to remain undisturbed in their illusions.

Abba Anthony said long ago, "There will come a time when all people will be crazy. And when they find someone who is not like them, they will pounce upon him, thrash him, and shriek: 'You are crazy, for you are not like us.'"

Hence, the "new human being," and every person in a process of changing into a "new human being," is and will remain utterly useless in this world. He lives as a very ordinary person. But his life is a life consistent with the unfathomable, mysterious will of the even more incomprehensible God, in His peace, and therefore fascinating. One cannot get away from this, as often as one may occasionally strive against it. This reality, concealed in the life of every Christian, assumes, among monks, an outer shape. It assumes primarily the shape of poverty, even of absolute destitution before God: the commonplace in which one can divine the uncommon. The process, in which every Christian is involved, becomes, for monks, a tangible form of life, as imperfect as this form may be. Thus monks do not experience anything different from all other Christians. But they experience it in a dissected, uncovered form, as it were, so that their brothers and sisters may perhaps learn something they can apply to their own lives.

# The Source of Inner Peace

*The Question of the Spiritual "Method"*

Ever since the arrival of the Far Eastern religions and forms of meditation in the West, people have been asking Christian monks about their own "methods" of meditation and centering. These questions have come at a time when monks do not live intensely and essentially from the deepest sources of their spiritual tradition. Nor have they ever practiced meditation techniques as demanding as, say, those of Zen monks. Christian monks are tempted to seek the reason in the decline and neglect of their own tradition. The urgent task was apparently to dig around in this Christian tradition and swiftly come up with appropriate, though forgotten, "methods." The job was done—albeit not primarily by monks—and, indeed, a few texts were unearthed, especially two by an English Carthusian of the fourteenth century. A new foreword was added, depicting and illustrating how to sit in a sensible Oriental position. This package was then marketed as a "precise introduction to contemplative meditation parallel to Zen." Other

Christian authors, especially in the Eastern Church (e.g., the Hesychasts, whose method of the "Jesus prayer" is now widely known thanks to "The Righteous Tales of a Russian Pilgrim"), contain possible elements and rudiments for a solid technique and methodology of concentration and stillness, which, if necessary, can be stylized into a "precise" method.

However, a survey, especially of the Western tradition, offers discouragingly lean pickings. In the perhaps 250,000 tightly spaced columns of the 220 volumes of Jacques Paul Migne's *Patrologia* (which incorporates the substance of all important Christian authors from the beginnings to the thirteenth century), there is not the least guidance of the sort that is offered by Yoga, Zen, Transcendental Meditation, and other schools of meditation today. One must therefore conclude that there was little need for or interest in a proper "technique" of concentration and meditation, and that, therefore, no universal method of achieving peace of mind was developed.

Furthermore, a narrower study of the sources leads one to the strange conclusion that the Christian monks had almost no sense of leisure and idleness; indeed, they were even suspicious of them.

### The "Busy Leisure" of the Christian Monks

If we start with the desert fathers, and continue through the great monastic rules until the late Middle Ages, one theme keeps recurring: a monk should avoid nothing so much as inactivity. For "idleness [*otiositas*] is the enemy of the soul," says Benedict in his rule. And Smaragdus, an influential Benedictine author of the ninth century, says, "All physical rest is an abomination [*abominatio est omnis corporalis requies*]." In Cassianus (ca. 360–435), who gave the West the tradition of the desert fathers, and in all monastic authors, it is easier to find urgent admonitions for constant work than appeals for free time.

One might think that at least the representatives of the most extreme form of eremitic life, the Recluses (who had themselves immured in a cell for the duration of their lives), would have developed a sense of idleness. But their rule, too, Grimlac's *Regula Solitariorum* of the ninth century, offers the clear–cut instruction: "They should not sit around in idle leisure [*non otio torpeant*]. . . . They should either sing psalms or devote themselves to Spiritual Reading or work with their hands, and observe the canonical hourly prayers with utter dedication."

Elsewhere, the "more contemplative" a cenobium is meant to be, the more planning goes into the order of each day and each life. (I am only pointing out this fact, not justifying it; it requires critical investigation.) The daily schedule of Carthusians, Trappists, or Carmelites was—and still is in part today—precisely regulated down to the last quarter hour. When individuals withdrew into an eremitic life, the first thing they did was set up a detailed daily agenda, thus developing a *"negotiotissimum otium,"* an "extremely busy leisure." This phrase is used by Paolo Giustiniani, the reformer of the Camaldoleses in the sixteenth century. In his rule for hermits, he writes:

> Everyone should try to devote a specific number of hours to working with his hands, and, during other established hours, to reading, praying, and other disciplines of the soul, and in such a way that the entire course of the day and the night seems short and too brief and there is always more left to do than there is time available. Woe to him who begins to find the days too long!

We moderns have the impression that Giustiniani was seeking and artificially creating for himself the kind of stress situation from which we are urgently trying to escape.

The Christian monastic tradition does have a rich literature on *otium*, otiosity, leisure. But, this usually does not refer to the kind of relaxed spare time and idleness that we have meant by "leisure" since the dawn of the Modern Age and Romanticism. *Otium* is not a state of physical and mental relaxation such as is practiced nowadays and can be precisely measured with biofeedback instruments.

Saint Bernard of Clairvaux once wrote to a friend, "I have experienced it, believe me: you find more in the forests than in books. Wood and stones will teach you about things that you cannot hear from the teachers." He was not alluding to a nature experience during a stroll through the forest or on a day off in the country. He was talking about an experience of heavy physical labor in field and forest, a kind of drudgery that he and many other monks, who were once the spoiled sons of nobility, must have found especially oppressive. It was during this strenuous labor, and not in quiet hours of idleness, that these monks sought and found their most intense spiritual experience. Nor is it a coincidence that, throughout the history of Christian monachism, physical labor always gained esteem in times of new spiritual awareness.

## The Spirituality of the Sermon on the Mount

Thus, if we slough off the heavy layer of prejudices and forms of expression that are products of their times, we do not come upon a spirituality of the privileged that demands, if one wishes to live in spiritual intensity, ideal circumstances like optimal conditions of architecture, time, silence, food, temperature, and humidity, such as are offered in modern (and expensive) meditation halls. What we find rather is the spirituality of the Sermon on the Mount. This is a spirituality for all people, a spirituality that promises the poor, the grieving, the hungering, the scorned and persecuted and reviled, the special experience of God's nearness (Matt. 5:3–13). This is not only in the sense of comforting the downtrodden by indicating their compensation in the afterlife, but as a gift in their painful situation. This is the mystical experience of the Apostle Paul, who, in the midst of affliction, experiences the strength of Christ and therefore "will all the more gladly boast of my weaknesses" (cf. 2 Cor. 12:9–10); who is "as dying, and behold we live; . . . as sorrowful, yet always rejoicing; as poor, yet making many rich; as having nothing, and yet possessing everything" (2 Cor. 6:9–10). Those who have been imprisoned and tortured for their religious convictions, those who, for the love of God, wear themselves out serving the poor and sharing their life— those people are presumably a lot closer to such an experience than the meditation experts who try to create as many alpha waves in their brains as possible because, according to William Johnston, "all contemplation is based on alpha."

This is the mystical *ec-stasy* [i.e., standing out] of Jesus Christ Himself into the will of the Father, His taking of Himself in obedience, in His entire existence, intensified to the utmost at Gethsemane and Golgotha; a final "rest" in the most extreme surrender and despair, beyond all physical and mental states.

Around 1200, the poet of the pentecostal sequence *Veni, Sancte Spiritus* reduced this experience to a pregnant formula:

> *In labore requies,*
> *in aestu temperies,*
> *in fletu solatium.*

> [In our labor, rest most sweet;
> graceful coolness in the heat;
> solace in the midst of woe.]

Special heed in these verses should be paid to the preposition *in.* It designates the paradoxical situation of rest *in* (not *after*) unrest, of coolness *in* (not *after*) the heat, of solace *in* (not *after*) woe. Not coincidentally, this stanza is in a song to the Holy Spirit, the *person-al* relationship between the Father and the Son. Such rest is based on an unrescindable *relatedness* to someone and is not a mental state *in itself.* In the midst of affliction, in the midst of stress, and in the midst of a psychological state of despair, there is a mysterious sostenuto, a transcendental "rest in the grace of mutual love" (as the twelfth-century Cistercian Aelred of Rievaulx describes the sense of security in a spiritual friendship).

Measured against today's meditational literature, the writers in the Christian tradition seem unpleasantly dogmatizing and moralistic. There have been many attempts at combing their works, as well as works in the mystical tradition of all religions, in order to distill the most effective methods for achieving a "mystical" state and thus to release these thinkers from their apparent historical limitations. But such undertakings violate them, for it is precisely in this peculiarity that they are true to the New Testament. Leisure, silence, peace and quiet, absorption: these are not specifically Christian values and categories. Nor do the gospels ever indicate that Jesus methodically guided his disciples along such lines. Stillness and peace of heart are consequences of self-renunciation and humility, which a man learns in the imitation of Christ, according to what Jesus said: "Take my yoke upon you, and learn from me; for I am gentle and lowly in heart, and you will find rest for your souls" (Matt. 11:29). That is why Christian authors keep quoting this passage whenever they speak of rest.

The requirement of sober "commandment-keeping" for mystical knowledge and love is particularly distinct and frequent in the Johannine writings: all this is a "hard saying" (John 6:60). How prosaic and disappointing the long list of Benedict's "Tools of Spiritual Art" (in chapter four of his rule) must be for anyone whose appetite for spiritual experience has been whetted by countless seductive book titles! Yet it has to be this way. We know the contemporary tendency to relativize dogmatics on the basis of certain theologically universal laws and methods and to seek states of consciousness per se. Contrary to this trend, the goal of Christian spirituality is to hold to the unmistakably unique Jesus Christ and to relate to Him. Only through this relationship in the Holy Spirit does a person develop the strength to integrate all the fragments of his life into an organic whole and develop the kind of "rest" that is not a question of time and leisure, but rather a question of being sustained by an ultimate *meaning*. However, if this relationship and this ultimate meaning are lost, then all methods and exercises for attaining peace merely attack symptoms and do not heal at the root. *This* is the actual problem whose symptom is the restless, hectic quality of our era. It is not a problem of spare time, of recreational activity, of developing new forms of worship and celebration. It is a problem of unrelatedness, of meaninglessness and—one is almost embarrassed to say it today—it is a question of morality.

This is evident if one looks at the "conservative" Catholic writers of the first half of our century, who have been neglected, benevolently or condescendingly, by many modern critics (even Catholics). Reinhold Schneider, Georges Bernanos, and Gertrud von le Fort were capable of communicating a true mystagogy within the inner space of faith. Those "modern" authors who ("still") deal with Christian themes offer little more than fairly banal or trivial statements about the "relevance" of Jesus and His tidings for today. Such writers impart little about the experiences and problems of people who have begun to deal existentially with Christ as adult Christians in a postconciliar Church. Instead, they remain outside the front door, juggling allusions and possibilities and demands and taking aim at the Church in its preconciliar state. Modern writers seem to have a secret fear of being made sterile by virtue. They may achieve grand things on a formal level, but only at the price of trivializing their themes and statements. They expose an endless number of things, but perceive woefully little. They remove all the fig leaves, but never find a new innocence.

## Crisis of the Ability to Relate

Decades ago, Georges Bernanos showed rare clarity in exposing the roots of this evil and also demonstrating its abysmal depths. In his opinion, all subliminal diseases of the mind and the spirit are due to modern repression of and yearning for God. This cutting of the umbilical cord to God is tantamount to surrendering to the abyss, ultimately to hell. Relation and devotion are supplanted by a boundless, yet distant, curiosity. The cleanly swept house is then occupied by the demons of pride, of independence, of self-defense. They make it impossible for the person to remain in his home any longer because emptiness, nothingness, and self-hatred attack him from the inside.

> He has shaken off his past, but the future ahead of him is equally hollow and empty, a new lie that he must take upon himself, an equally great "boredom." Sensuality, that small change of hell, he has seen through long since; "he has the miser's scorn for this kind of squandering." Thus, he is deprived of all time, he has no living-space left, no dimension of hope.

> (The Bernanos quotations in this chapter are from H. U. von Balthasar, *Bernanos*, Cologne and Olten, 1954, pp. 334–76.)

Bernanos's country priest says:

> . . . And they have no conception of evil itself, of the enormous suction of emptiness, nothingness. If our human race is to perish, then the causes will be disgust and surfeit. The human person will be gradually gnawed up as a wooden beam is by its invisible mushrooms, which, in just a few weeks, can transform a solid piece of oak into a crumbling material that a finger can effortlessly pierce.

Man remains a person only in the magnetic field of a fundamental relationship. If he leaves this field of energy, he will crumble into bits, like iron filings when an electromagnet is switched off. This chaos, this disruption of relating, is the deepest cause of all disquiet and restlessness. Among all the reasons why countless forms of meditation are so popular nowadays, not the least may be that they do not presuppose the capacity for personal relationship. Letting go, reversing the process of becoming, as an exercise, strikes many contemporaries as easier and more desirable than letting oneself be taken and devoting oneself to a "thou."

All the symptoms of our era's disease, as depicted by Bernanos, are also disturbances of the human faculty for relating. *Lying* and *injustice* shatter elementary laws and deny the requirements of human existence both privately and socially. *Sexuality*, good in itself as a gift of God, is perverted into the three-dimensional language of abuse

> because this fugue of human nature, in which the physical can and should become the manifestation of spiritual love, contains all possibilities of concealment (instead of manifestation), perversion (instead of immediate devotion), abuse of love itself, and hence the disintegration of the core of the person. . . . Thus, the sexual act becomes an inducement to display the contradictions of sin, of spiritual egotism. . . . Falling upon each other to have a pleasure that is already surpassed in lust itself and has already become boredom.

*Homosexuality* is "the phenomenon of a perversion of love for one's own sex, that is, for one's own loving essence: inversion becomes the metaphor of a love that closes back upon itself [if the word *love* makes any sense here]," total self-relatedness and self-enjoyment in the mirror of the other. *Drugs* (in Bernanos, morphium)

> are the quasi-sacramental act that denies the divine hope for grace and, instead, reaches mightily for an inaccessible Eden. It is the metaphor for the fact that the sinner has given up the search for reality—beyond the dream existence of this life—and replaced it with the search for the desired dream of pleasure. It is the flight from the dreadful tedium of godlessness into an "artificial paradise."

Aldous Huxley, in discussing the severe asceticism of contemplation in earlier times, for instance that of the Vicar of Ars, sees it as a striving toward

> creating the internal conditions favorable to spiritual insight. When they were not starving themselves into low blood sugar and a vitamin deficiency, or beating themselves into intoxication by histamine, adrenalin, and decomposed protein, they were cultivating insomnia and praying for long periods in uncomfortable positions in order to create the psycho-physical symptoms of stress. In the intervals they sang interminable psalms, thus increasing the amount of carbon dioxide in the lungs and the blood stream, or, if they were Orientals, they did breathing exercises to accomplish the same purpose.
> (*Doors of Perception and Heaven and Hell* [New York: Harper & Row, 1954], p. 155)

Today, Huxley feels, the same effect can be achieved more simply and more quickly by the proper use of drugs —and, naturally, one can also omit the entire theological superstructure: the call to imitation, the *Imitatio Christi*, the ideal of becoming uniform with the self-surrendering Jesus Christ, an ideal that is the motive force of every truly serious Christian asceticism, appears as a negligible quantity.

What Huxley expresses in a particularly obvious fashion, is simply a monstrous misreading of the Christian mystical tradition, a misreading that is widespread today in subtler forms—the confusion between the essence (the relationship with Christ) and the accident (the experience of any states that might result, but need not; for us here the state of inner stillness and peace) to the point of discarding the essence in favor of this accident.

*Love for Christ*

Let us therefore return to our monks who so disagreeably dogmatize and moralize.

The Russian starets Macarius of Optina once wrote to a man seeking counsel: "If, with everything you do, you achieve no spiritual gain but only internal disquiet, than it is clear that you do not have humility." Humility is that inner stance of selflessness, of service, of disregard of oneself and release from oneself, which comes from, and is made possible by, emulating the life of Jesus Christ. Thus, one can extrapolate from the words of the starets Macarius: "If you have inner disquiet, then it is clear that you orient yourself too little by Jesus Christ, that you ask too little what happened to *Him,* that you care too little about sharing *His fate.*"

It was from here that the mystics in the Christian tradition found their way to peace; and it was from *this* source that their creative forces were nourished for shaping a Christian existence. Out of the strength of their relationship to Christ, the monks shaped a complicated, demanding lifestyle that receives unity and wholeness purely from this root. This relationship is, so to speak, the soul of the body of their outer form of life. It would make little sense to remove individual elements from this totality, this practice of life, and, having sliced them out, transmit them to others as a method for a quiet life.

I write these words so resolutely not from a position of strength, but from one of my own weakness. For in today's monasteries, this "soul" is threatened (as it surely has been at all times) if a consistent focus on God and the teachings of Jesus Christ and His Gospel are no longer the living creative principle of the monastic community—if, instead, traditional rules and patterns of behavior or innerworldly compulsions and (perhaps quite good and pious) goals and tasks and calculations become dominant. In that case, the body will crumble into its individual parts, and all the new opportunities for relaxation and leisure and vacation, all the innovative possibilities of meditation, will not help to keep the body together as an organic whole. The line between being possessed by the demon of activism and feeling the ecstasy of a totally serving devotion is as thin as the razor's edge. The same can be said for the line between a focusing on God in pure existence and a circling around oneself in aesthetic idleness and absorption.

The Christian out in the "world," from the very start, lives in circumstances and conditions that have nothing to do with God and Jesus Christ. When he feels inner disquiet, it would no doubt be simpleminded to seek the defect *only* in the individual's own lack of humility. The fault lies *also* in the structures and relationships and rhythms created by non-humble people and to which he is exposed.

People today ask whether the heritage of Christian monachism can help free them from the disquiet and malaise into which they are cast. In response to this question, I cannot offer anything immediately practical. Nor do I really care to. I would much rather stress the decisive, essential point on which we must focus before undertaking anything practical: we have to seek a cure and not just treat symptoms so that we end up going in circles around ourselves.

The Occidental monk who dominates iconography is a man with a book: the Christian monk reads a book or writes a book. He lives from Another and toward Another. That is where he has found his "rest." Saint Bernard of Clairvaux liked to hold up the example of earlier popes to Pope Eugene III:

> They found leisure in the worst turbulence. The city
> was beleaguered, and the sword of the barbarians lay

> on the necks of the inhabitants. This did not deter the
> holy Pope Gregory from penning texts full of spiritual
> wisdom in peace and quiet, for it was at this very time
> that he wrote, with utmost care and in a polished style,
> his commentary on the most obscure and most difficult
> part of the Book of Ezekiel.

Such is the "practical" advice of the Christian tradition: in extreme danger, do the simple, immediately necessary things with care. And seek your support in the Word of God. It may be dry bread that you must chew for a long time before it will yield any taste and nourishment, but seek in it a living relationship to God, to Jesus Christ. Seek in it the God who loves us and who became one of us.

Rather timidly, I have spoken again and again of the "relationship" to Jesus Christ. Now, in conclusion, I would like to speak of the *love* for Jesus Christ. This love alone will help us. To try to find the meaning of life in the form of an ideological system where everything has its place will not suffice: all who think purely in terms of dogma will fail. A sufficient meaning for life is also not to be found in the form of moral instructions or psychological techniques: the moral apostles and meditation masters will fail. All that can help us is a new love that reaches all levels of our being. Love makes even the most complicated and most confused things simple. The creative strength and imagination of love is immense.

> Love bears all things, believes all things . . . endures all
> things. Love never ends; as for prophecies, they will
> pass away; as for tongues, they will cease; as for knowl-
> edge, it will pass away. . . . For now we see in a mirror
> dimly, but then face to face. Now I know in part; then
> I shall understand fully, I have been fully known. So
> faith, hope, love, these three; but the greatest of these
> is love (1 Cor. 13:7–8, 12–13).

# The Grief and Joy of Christians

## *"They Should Look More Redeemed"*

Not too long ago, an American magazine ran a story about a priest who had removed all effigies of the Crucified Man from his church and replaced them with pictures of the Resurrected Christ. He explained to his parishioners that it was time we Christians put our pascal faith at the center and no longer talked so much about the cross and suffering, but rather more about the joy of the redeemed.

We can hardly assume that this iconographic break with a tradition of two thousand years will come into vogue. But the intent and action of this clergyman are worth examining. Upon closer inspection, we find they are symptomatic of a malaise that present-day Christians feel about themselves and their faith. Nietzsche's provoking, ironic, and, I might say, seductive cry "They should look more redeemed, the Redeemed!" has been unsettling Christians since it was first uttered. "You must look more redeemed," the mother superior admonishes the sister who walks down the corridor with a dismal mien. "You should be men of joy!" the priest on the ambo urges members of the congregation who look weary and burdened. "We've got to cultivate more joy and cheer," the curate says to himself and plans the next teenage dance in the parish hall, because that's the best way to get young people here. The devotees of the charismatic renewal show us in practice how cheery and peppy a spirit-filled Christianity can be. Joy, enthusiasm, experience of redemption—these are expected of Christians today if they are to have credibility. And they expect it of themselves. Christian periodicals have been harping on this theme for the past few years: we Christians must rediscover joy if we do not wish to belie our glad tidings and condemn them to ineffectiveness.

But is it really so certain that every Christian committed to a life of faith can, indeed must, radiate joy? Is not *the* symbol of Christianity now and always the cross, the image of the Redeemer nailed to the cross, and not a serenely smiling Buddha? And what about Mary, the most shining model for believers, the woman whom God truly, indeed physically, "seized?" Has not Christian art for centuries depicted her chiefly as the Pietà, the Mother of Sorrows?

## Faith: No Simple Way of Looking Cheerful

There is the sadness of the tired, lukewarm, half-hearted Christians who do not live in the freedom of the sons of God, but as morose servants more or less resigned to God's will. This sadness is truly bad. It is caused by lack of faith, lack of consistency, lack of depth. It is the sign of a troubled, narrow, selfish heart—a heart that sees only its own limited possibilities and therefore becomes despondent instead of believing in God's endless possibilities and remaining hopeful and confident. Yet throughout the centuries, and also in the most recent times, many excellent things have been written about this sadness, which the ancients called *acedia*.

Now, however, I wish to speak about a different kind of Christian sadness: the sorrow of the person who takes the risk of faith; the pain and suffering of the person who has set out upon the Imitation of Christ. I want to try and show that the thesis that living faith and visible joy belong together does not hold in the naive sense in which it is often presented. Maintained or unthinkingly assumed, it is unrealistic and will tend to evoke despair rather than courage in many earnest Christians. Such Christians are forced into the dichotomous role of the clown, who is supposed to spread joy and merriment no matter what his heart may feel. If they give in to this coercion, the result is a cheery Christian theater and a sentimental mood, not an authentic Christian existence. We must recognize that many Christians are *not* relaxed and externally cheerful, especially those who plunge deep into their faith. It is hard for us to accept this fact, for what is the sense of a faith that cannot produce tangibly positive results?

The natural sciences have accustomed us to demonstrating the truth and correctness of a process through experimental procedures. We tend to transpose these methods to the spiritual life: under given conditions, a certain result must come about within a specific length of time. So if we presuppose genuine faith and a healthy human sensibility, we would expect to get a cheerful, balanced human being or a "transcendental experience" or at least some sort of registrable positive result. If the result is not forthcoming, then something is wrong with the premise. Either faith is defective or the person in question has a pretty bad neurosis. Whoever seeks the roots of the failure of the experiment will, of course, tend to blame the exceedingly unfavorable laboratory conditions: his environment and the adverse circumstances of his life.

Unfortunately, in the area of faith there is no such infallible procedure and proof. This creates a problem, especially since, nowadays, Eastern religions and forms of meditation offer apparently more efficient methods of achieving a balanced psyche and profound "experiences." Anyone indulging in just a bit of Transcendental Meditation can physically measure the lightning-fast positive results on his brain currents and his nervous system. We would love to have something similar for our faith.

But if you get involved with our God, then you are letting yourself in for an adventure with unpredictable consequences. There is no way of calculating what the ultimate result will be—at least not what it will be in *this* life.

### Faith That Makes Us Like Christ in His Entire Fate

The German theologian Hans Urs von Balthasar recently published an article, "The Peculiarity of Christian Mysticism" (in Balthasar & Haas: *Grundfragen der Mystik*, Einsiedeln, 1974, pp. 57ff.), that is very helpful to our discussion. As he points out, on the road to faithful obedience according to the model of Christ:

> . . . there is the decisive maxim that it is not the *experience* of union with God that is the yardstick of perfection, but rather *obedience*, which, in the experience of abandonment by God, can be just as closely tied to God as in the experience of union. While the synoptic Jesus

on the cross utters the cry of abandonment, the Johannine Jesus says: "The hour is coming, indeed it has come, when you . . . will leave me alone; yet I am not alone, for the Father is with me" (John 16:32). With me in abandonment exactly as in the felt union. Thus, the Christian walking the path of his Master is not promised any immediate (mystical) experience of God. The servant should be content if he goes through what his master went through (Matt. 10:25), far more—as the final point of his earthly career—a configuration like the crucified Lord (thus the promise to Peter in John 21:18f). . . . The Church and in it the Christian [are] made similar to the entire fate of Christ: crucified with him, buried with him, resurrected with him, ascended with him—according to Paul's words. Whether one aspect or the other of this imitation in the life of a Christian or of the Church as a whole comes to the fore is not within human discretion, but within the sole providence of the paternal will, which has the sole right to know the time and the hour, hence also the duration of time and the hour, for example the length of an epoch of internal darkness.

If one now postulates that a Christian who lives in true faith has to be a cheerful Christian, then one blindly assumes that only the experience of Easter joy is a mature, authentic experience of faith. But this is onesided and unrealistic. According to Hans Urs von Balthasar, "the notion, which prevailed until recently in Carmelite cloisters, that a truly perfect soul must die in an ecstasy of love" is false.

Precisely in term of the cross, it seems at least equally suitable that the soul—like the prioress in Bernanos's *Dialogues des Carmélites*—should die in a dreadful ecstasy of fear, quite "unedifying" for everyone around. . . . Never does a Christian leave the cross behind him; never can he know whether God does not wish to pull

> him back into the Dark Night. . . . The most eloquent
> image of little Thérèse is the "plaything" that a human
> being would like to be for the infant Jesus, a ball for him
> to throw, squeeze to his heart, but also pierce holes in,
> or merely let lie.

Thus, one cannot unilaterally make the "joyous" saints, as, for example, Saint Philip Neri or Don Bosco, the epitome of Christian holiness and credibility—or form an arbitrary image of the saints. How completely false and historically incorrect is, for instance, the cliché of the animal lover and Brother Evercheer that has covered up the figure of Saint Francis of Assisi! One need only compare the faces in the early portraits of the saint at Subiaco and at Assisi to see the gap separating him from all the preachers of Franciscan happy-go-lucky joie de vivre. In those early portraits, Francis is more like the serious saints of icons and the careworn Brother Nicholas of Flüe.

## The Call to Sym-pathize, Com-miserate, Suffer With Christ

Joy that is visible to all, contagious for all, is a charisma, a gracious gift from God. There are people who receive it. But Jesus also has disciples who now mourn and weep, and he calls them blessed because some day they shall laugh (Matt. 5:4; par. Luke 6:21). The ancients knew of the "gift of tears," of the "contrition of the heart." Benedict wants his monks always to go about "with lowered heads" and to "avoid laughter." One should not misinterpret this as a duty to be sorrowful and to vegetate. On the contrary, it can express a call to *com-miserate,* to suffer along with the wretchedness and imperfection of the world. This is the frame of mind that Reinhold Schneider delineates in his *Winter in Vienna*. A man who has totally surrendered to God can be plunged by Him into an abyss of suffering and wretchedness. Then all bromides about the joy of faith must falter. They can even increase this man's misery by boring the thorn of doubt—doubt in the authenticity of his faith—into his flesh.

Influenced by our long tradition and, more recently, by the meditation movement, we facilely imagine the spiritual and psychological disposition of mankind in a schema limited to the individual. If a man has gone through a certain period of maturity and testing in the life of faith, he ought to experience something like a "breakthrough." From then on in his life, the experience of joy ought to dominate over the experiences of pain and grief. Reality, however, is altogether different.

In the spiritual development of a Christian, joy can predominate during the early period; and then, the deeper he launches into the Imitation of Christ, the heavier the cross can weigh upon him. The experience of darkness and difficulty in a Christian's life is not simply the means and the phase of his purging and purification, the threshold to a personal experience of light and joy. It can also be—and very often is—participation in the Passion of Christ, involvement in the sufferings of the Lord, which continues in His limbs until the end of history. This is so because no one reaches God "privately." The individual is a member of the community and of the body of the Church, which develops through the centuries as a totality, passing through heights and depths and being purified until she can finally be conceived as the flawless "bride of the lamb" (Apoc. 21). That is why spiritually profound, "progressive" people can be so potently summoned to this experience of purging, a *collective* purging that far surpasses the measure and necessity of their individual purification and becomes a sharing in the moans and sighs of all Creation. Christian perfection in this earthly life does not mean having already passed through the suffering and being above it. The "perfect" man is sent over and over again with Christ into the very midst of suffering.

## Growing in Faith and in the Ability to Suffer Along

Growth in faith increases human sensibility—both positively and negatively. For the saints, infinite realms of joy are opened; but they, too, suffer the worst for their own sake and for the unredeemed sins of the world. With the ability to envision the coming, incipient glory of the Messiah, insight into the depths of the abyss of evil and godlessness also increases. The scales of feeling are loaded more heavily on both sides; and thus the scales do not necessarily tip on the side of joy. This lends the believer's life an enormous tension, which he sometimes can barely endure.

Measured by this experience, much of what is offered as an example of "Christian joy" can be considered too easy and misleading. Think of the members of a Christian sect who march through a hospital, plucking guitars; they are almost pushy in their happiness (thanks to Jesus' love) as they tell all the patients about how they are saved. More credible is the cancer patient who, though also touched by Jesus' love, does not laugh, or even smile, but rather bears his illness bravely and inconspicuously. Indeed, according to Scripture, the faith of the lamenting Job is far more solid than that of his "enlightened" friends, who are "joyous in faith," and who quite simply lack any faculty for deeper emotions.

I strongly doubt whether the cheery, merry, peppy, piously free Christianity that we may secretly envy in today's sects will be capable of providing new brilliance for the glad tidings. Is it not enough that an eternally smiling human race without fellow suffering, *com-miseration,* beams at us from posters and magazine covers? The ever-cheery Christian could easily become a trivial variant of this cliché. The man who, for the love of Christ, weeps with those who are now doomed to weep could more readily give them an inkling of the nearness and *commiseration* of our God than the man whose unabashed laughter makes them feel misunderstood, even ridiculed.

In a century or two, historians and theologians will be able to survey our era more effectively from a distance than we can today. Perhaps they will say that, during the second half of the century, we Christians in the West talked a lot about the misery and suffering of the other two-thirds of humanity and that we did a little to relieve their wretchedness. But, at bottom, they did not touch our hearts. Instead, for our domestic use, we concocted a theology of playing, of unabashed fun and joie de vivre. They may wonder how we could possibly realize to what extent we misused theology to justify our Christianity of prosperity.

A committed Christian is basically no gladder and no sadder than any other person; but both his gladness and his sadness are more intense. The difficulty remains that we cannot *prove* our faith in a clear-cut way, or gauge its efficiency with the methods of empirical social research. Our life is and will be for quite a while a life "hid with Christ in God" (Col. 3:3).

## The Hidden, Concealed Joy

Does this mean that a Christian's life, lived consistently, would not have to produce the "fruits of the Holy Spirit," love, joy, and peace (cf. Gal. 5:22), i.e., something that can be experienced? Of course not. But we must not expect these fruits on too shallow a stratum of life. It is heartwarming to meet a cheerful, relaxed, believing person who radiates optimism and confidence. But who can say how much of it he owes simply to his happy nature or to a naiveté that spares him confrontation with questions that may trouble another man, whose faith is at least equally deep?

And vice versa. Who can say how much hidden suffering and how much quietly borne loneliness and wretchedness this outwardly cheerful person has endured or must secretly endure over and over again? And who can say that an outwardly careworn person who looks tense and unredeemed, does not know joy? His joy may be very deeply hidden. Perhaps it is only a pebble under a mountain of suffering and skepticism—a final certainty, in the midst of darkness, that his condition must be *thus* and not otherwise, and that it *thus* has its meaning, albeit ungraspable and ineffable. His certainty can be a realization that is bare and naked and does not reach feeling and emotion: the joy of the fish at being caught in God's net, and yet a writhing and struggling with all the fibers of its being against the death that must be died. We should not be surprised that a person who experiences *this* kind of joy may seem a lot tenser on the outside than a person for whom the life of faith is a kind of life insurance policy—he acquires an ultimate certitude with relatively small payments—and who therefore radiates a balanced and carefree demeanor.

However, we should not leap to any false conclusions either.

The Christian can have a calling to participate very intensely in the passion of his Master, as I have already explained. However, we who are *post Christum natum* and *post Christum passum et resurrectum* can never fall again into the abyss of lonely suffering and dying into which Christ plunged. Since His descent into hell, the power of hell is broken, and He is there with His disciple, no, His disciple is even all the more one with Him the deeper he plunges. This disciple also "knows" and "experiences" it. I have put both verbs in quotation marks, because this "knowing" and this "experiencing" are beyond our comprehension and perception, as it were, and can be reduced to a final unthinkable and unfeelable sostenuto. However, this kind of "joy," which can be shrouded in great sorrow, is not something that such a person will wish to exchange for any other joy. And it will be perceptible to anyone around him who has a feel for it. For one really needs a special feel. It can't be found for sale to everyone in the marketplace.

# A Holy Saturday Experience

Some friends and I were talking about which day of the Church year we felt closest to in terms of our experiences and emotions. One man's favorite holiday was Christmas, with its warmth, its lights, and its tidings of goodwill and God's closeness. Another found his basic Christian experience on Easter Monday, with its Gospel of the road to Emmaus. A third recognized himself and his situation best in the nine days between Christ's Ascension and Pentecost, the time when the Lord left His near and dear and all waited in prayer for the promised Holy Spirit.

During this conversation, I realized that, for several years, "my" day has been Holy Saturday. This is the day on which I feel most deeply my experience of God and the world and my calling. This could change some day, and the inseparable whole of our world of faith might then open up to me from a different point of view. But for now, Holy Saturday is the most intense expression of what I live on and how I live in faith. When I grew more conscious of this, I found that several problems and issues of faith confronting many Christians today—often very urgently and anxiously—gained a deeper meaning, revealing themselves as a particularly intense way of living in union with Christ. This inkling that the apparent absence and silence of God might be a concentrated form of his nearness and his essential communication had something of an Easter liberation for me. I felt an urge to "go quickly and tell [my] brethren" (Matt. 28: 7–10). Such was my frame of mind when writing the following pages.

Well-known authors such as Adrienne von Speyr, Hans Urs von Balthasar, and Karl Rahner wrote about Holy Saturday years ago; their work was theologically thorough and systematic. I deliberately did *not* re-read them before setting out to formulate the following, for I do not wish to develop a systematically rounded "spirituality of Holy Saturday." I quite simply want to describe what dawned upon me about the mystery of Holy Saturday, how I can live from it in faith, and what questions or indications I found in it. Perhaps my experiences can aid a few people to grasp more deeply the secret of their lives and faith. Perhaps, in an altogether prosaic situation that is seemingly remote from God, they will be amazed to realize, "Surely the Lord is in this place; and I did not know it" (Gen. 28:16). This was what happened to the patriarch Jacob who, when fleeing his brother, slept on bare stone, unprotected, out in the open. Unexpectedly, it was revealed to him that he was abiding in the house of God and standing at the gates of heaven.

## The Day of Naked Reality and Silence

On the high feasts of the Christian year, in fact at every celebration of the mass, I am troubled by a certain helplessness at perceiving what is being celebrated and at letting myself be profoundly seized and marked by it. I always feel at the mercy of realities that surpass my understanding. This occurs above all during Holy Week and Easter Week. For a time, I almost feared these weeks: this abyss of passion and this upswing of Easter jubilation, this sorrow and this joy, which I had to overcome rather than experience and endure.

Between these two weeks, however, comes Holy Saturday, a day without sorrow and without joy. It is the day of austerity and exposure. Our monastery church, normally void of pictures and restricted to essentials, is even further stripped of all decoration on this day. The altar block stands rude and naked in space; and in lieu of candles, only the sharp, empty thorns of the holders gape out. The uncolored light falling through the high windows strikes only the bare elements of stone and wood. The liturgy of this day is correspondingly simple, limited to the pulse beat of the horary prayers, speaking of a kind of peace and calm that I am able to grasp.

Everything on this day strikes me as genuine—more so than on any other day of the year. There are no pictures here that disguise reality; nothing is celebrated here that my experience cannot deal with; there is no bombast to stoke the flames of my distrust, my doubt, my critical spirit: no dramatization of any suffering and no transfiguration of any victory, but only the fact of my own presence between death and resurrection. Here, quite simply, life is endured as it is, suspended between an ungraspable Good Friday and an incomprehensible Easter. Here, time stands still for an instant and does not exact too much sorrow or too much joy from me. Here is the Sabbath, the Sabbath of my own life. Here, I do not have to suffer anything or reexperience it for myself: I can simply abandon myself to reality and *exist, here.*

What I feel for the liturgy, I also experience with the dramas and feasts of life in general: a vast helplessness in regard to grasping them. In the light of the immense suffering that people experience in our century and that we know about all too well (unlike the people of earlier times), what else am I to feel here, what else am I to say here? Is it really possible to get spiritually involved in so many human tragedies? Or must we necessarily die the "living death of the feelings?" Must we shed that part of our consciousness that includes reports and impressions of other people's sufferings in order to continue living?

On Holy Saturday, I sense a different possibility: the chance to settle in a deep place where all the sorrow of the world flows together and becomes something that is no longer sorrow, but rather a wordless and emotionless hereness and withness that looks like death.

Holy Saturday is the day of wept-out eyes: no tears are left. It is the day after the pain: the suffering has gone beyond its high point and its utmost threshold of tolerance. Pain and absence of pain now come together. This is the day of numbness: it contains neither joy nor sorrow, for joy has lost its credibility or is not yet attainable, and sorrow is no longer to be grasped. It is the day of wordlessness: all words are worn, they sound like claptrap, they cannot help, they can only cover up. It is the day without prayers: for even the Word of the Father is hushed in its radical surrender. Holy Saturday is the day of the zero point, when I can only say, and only have to say: "Yes, this is how it is."

## In the Innermost Depth of Life

There is a sorrow from the depth of the world that is like a bottomless lake, which, if a man leans over it, threatens to pull him down deeper and deeper and swallow him up in his abyss. I feel the sorrow of Holy Saturday differently. It is a hushing into a peace without emotion or experience —but a peace all the same. Reinhold Schneider once described it as follows when he wrote about Saint John of the Cross:

> When he committed all sorrow into God's hands, he grew calm; he saw the sufferings doled out among people like mysterious coins whose value is revealed only in the afterlife. And whatever seemed wicked pointed up to its concealed meaning. . . . Did this existence not contain the entire substance of life? He lived as though at the bottom of the sea, no longer attainable by men and indifferent to everything that they might devise against him, but imbued with a peace that balanced the share in the goods of the world. Only now did he feel, shuddering, that poverty is the most delightful property; that in the innermost depth of life, values change, and that which men have called nothingness contains the highest good. (*Der fünfte Kelch* [Cologne, 1953] p. 25f.)

An existence in which the entire substance of life is enclosed, its immense variety compressed into a kernel without taste, a Host; living as though at the bottom of the sea, in total poverty, in the innermost depth of life, existing in what people call nothingness. This description, I found, articulated the essence of my calling as a monk and what I experience in it: this inability to grasp anything adequately, this desire to understand and this incapacity for understanding, this hunger and thirst for God, this passion that changes more and more into a kind of dying and numbness before Him.

## An Experience of Dying

Once, I lay down on my cot in the hermitage and ima- gined that this was the moment of my death. I lay there in the same position that someday I would be lying in on my deathbed in the middle of the chancel. In concentric circles, my mind detached itself from everything and moved inward—away from the universe, from my sur- roundings, from my plans, friends, and anxieties, from my sensory impressions, from my body—until, in a deep still- ness and loneliness, only a tiny dot of myself remained, motionless, timeless, spaceless. It would only have taken a tiny step to reduce it to zero and let it slide through the narrow needle's eye of annihilation—where to? I sensed an ungraspable new world, endlessly vast, in an absolute silence and clarity. But this was only premonition, not experience.

Did this have anything at all to do with God, or was it merely a psychological drill, a questionable self–reduction to a state of unconsciousness where one can forget the world and God? Ramón Lull points to such a possibility in *Of the Lover and the Beloved:* "Sleep overcame the lover, for he had sought his beloved until he was weary. And he lay in fear of forgetting his beloved. He wept to keep from sinking into sleep and losing the remembrance of his beloved."

Jan van Ruysbroeck, in *The Adornment of the Spiritual Marriage,* lucidly and graphically describes a dubious form of coming to rest:

All creatures tend by nature to rest, and that is why rest is sought by the good and the bad in manifold ways.

But mind you: If a man is bare and imageless by his senses and idle, inactive by the supreme powers, then he quite naturally comes to rest. And all creatures can find this rest and possess it in a purely natural state without inducement of God's grace if they merely empty themselves of images and release themselves from all manner of activity. The loving man, however, can find no rest here, for the love and the internal touching of God's grace never rest, and that is why the ardent man in his interior cannot remain for long in [purely] natural rest.

But now observe the way in which this natural rest is cultivated. One sits still without practice, either mental or physical, in idleness, merely so that the state of rest may begin and remain undisturbed. However, the rest practiced in this way is not permitted, for it makes man blind in ignorance and idly self-absorbed. And this rest is merely an idleness into which man falls, forgetting himself, as well as God and all things, when he is supposed to be active. This rest is the opposite of the supernatural rest, which one possesses in God, for this supernatural rest is a loving melting, with a simple look into the incomprehensible light. This rest is God, which is always actively striven for in ardent yearning, found in enjoying affection, and eternally possessed in the melting of love, and which, once possessed, is nevertheless always striven for, this rest is so sublimely high above natural rest, just as God is sublime over all creatures.

And that is why people are deceived if they seek themselves, if they fall into natural rest, and neither seek God with desire nor find him with enjoying love. For the rest they have resides in a deprivation of themselves, to which they tend by nature and habit. And in this natural rest, one cannot find God; however, it does lead men to an unattachedness that both pagans and Jews can find, like all human beings, no matter how evil they are, to the extent that they live on in their sins without remorse and can free themselves from images and all manner of activity. In this unattachedness, rest is pleasurable and great. This [kind of rest] is not a sin per se, for it is by nature in all men to the extent that they can unattach themselves. But if one wishes to practice it and achieve it without the works of virtue, then a man will fall into spiritual pride and into a self–complacency from which one very seldom recovers. And at times, such a man imagines that he already has and is that to which he can never attain. Thus, if a man possesses that rest in false unattachment, and every loving turn strikes him as an obstruction, he will remain trapped in his rest per se and live in contradiction to the . . . manner that unites man with God, and this is the start of all spiritual confusions.

## Two Forms of Nonexperience

There are two forms of nonexperience, rest and night, which can easily be confused with one another. One comes about when a person pulls in all feelers and antennae of perception, communication, emotion, and love, reducing himself to a "nothingness" or, in any event, to an isolated monad. The other comes about when a person stretches these feelers and antennae of perception and communication, of emotion and love, so far out that they break and disintegrate because of the excess of experience. Either way, this state and this space of emptiness, of total stillness, and "nothingness" contains "nothing." It is surrounded and qualified, however, by two very different forms of practical life and prayer. At the center, the core itself, it is difficult to distinguish between these two states. But from their access routes and their "outskirts," their specific natures can be very clearly determined.

I have stopped placing myself in the situation of death, as described earlier, because I wonder if this is fruitful and if this exercise might not develop a very specific suction effect toward that questionable "natural" rest that van Ruysbroeck speaks of. Indeed, I wonder if it is not a temptation to be so presumptuous as to play with, fiddle around with, one's own death, with this event that is out of man's control. In Dostoievsky's *The Possessed,* the engineer Kirilov commits suicide in order to seize God's mastery over death. In our times, Jean Améry has propagated and practiced the right freely to take one's own life, as the extreme privilege and hallmark of dignity for human freedom and autonomy in regard to the unpredictable. This is the ultimate consequence of reversing the attitude of a loving availability and giving of self to the gesture of defiant hurling of self and proud independence, which may be secretly and subliminally involved in many forms of meditative exercise and letting–go, in many attempts to deal with the unavailable by using methods and techniques to make it available. This is not meant to cast suspicion on all methodical practices of meditation and silence. They make sense and are justified if they assist ready devotion and presentness. But it is crucial to recognize their limits.

## The Innermost Core of the Self

One thing has become very clear to me from this experience: in all my seeking for God and men, the essence is and must be not to do or experience just *anything*, but to devote myself to God and men with that innermost, naked core of my being, the core that I have sensed in this exercise.

Most of what we usually experience and perform, in both the love of fellow men and the love of God, operates on a superficial level. We give away *something* of ourselves—our feelings, our thoughts, our bodies, our goods, our time, our work energy—but not really *ourselves*. We do not have ourselves in hand; we cannot—and often we do not wish to—give ourselves away. If we are sincere, then all the *things* we give away ought to express our willingness to give *ourselves* away. Indeed, they ought indirectly to affect that core of our being that we cannot grasp and influence directly; and they ought to affect it in such a way that this core is seized in the movement of giving and provides the giving with its actual depth, endurance, and essentiality. But this core of our being seems to be highly indolent and immovable. It takes a huge number of gestures, deeds, and utterances of love, devotion, and service on the level of conscious everyday life to draw that core along in the depth of unconsciousness and make it change essentially. Even such an utterly radical saint as Nicholas of Flüe evidently went through this experience, which he formulated in his prayer: "Lord, take me from myself and give me totally to you!" Even though he uncompromisingly surrendered his entire existence to God, he felt that only God Himself could induce his heavy, self-willed self to experience this surrender in its depths and ultimately to perceive it.

God cares not so much about the many words of our prayers (cf. Matt. 6:7–8) as about this essential surrender of our selves. Words—sometimes even the *many* words— exist more for our sake than God's. They have their meaning when they permeate us and open our beings to God, all the way down to the depths, to the very core. But words always have their danger too. They can become self-sufficient and an end, a work, a pleasure, unto themselves, and ultimately replace the surrender of the being. When I think of the five hours I spend in choral prayers every day, they seem like a huge mountain of sand that I drag over to God. Now and then, they contain a few very tiny golden motes of genuine surrender and devotion—and only these few grains are essential. They emerge quite unpredictably. Unfortunately, there is no method to filter them out in advance, to present only them, and thereby to spare myself the trouble of dragging along all the sand they are concealed in. Hence, this persistent, helpless gesture of dragging is an important task. It is to be hoped that it keeps reaching deeper and deeper into my being, down to its deepest strata, so that I really become someone who —consciously, unconsciously, subconsciously—never does, or wishes to do, anything but drag himself to God and, along with himself, all the people in whom he has a share and who are connected with him.

## From the Sign to the Reality

Holy Saturday strikes me as the day on which gestures, ceremonies, practices, prayers, and good thoughts—all the things we perform our reality with, but can also disguise it with—stop. On Holy Saturday, only this reality *itself* is left, wordless, imageless, experienceless: no more liturgy of suffering and dying, no process, no motion—only the sheer state of having died. There is nothing more to feel, to experience, to say. Not even a sacrament is celebrated. Recall the words sung in the Corpus Christi hymn: " . . . *et antiquum documentum novo cedat ritui";* the old, blood sacrifice of bulls and goats must give way to the new rite of the sacramental sacrifice of Christ. On Holy Saturday, this is demanded again, one level higher. Again, the "old" sacramental sacrifice must yield to the new, ultimate rite, which is no longer a rite: the reality of being sacrificed. Here, existence replaces rite and absorbs it by fulfilling it down to its final meaning. Just as, for a still unbaptized man who professes Christ, the martyrdom of the "blood baptism" replaces the water baptism, what the baptismal rite communicates in the sign—the act of being taken into the death and resurrection of Christ—is imparted to this martyr existentially by his completely "unliturgical" death. Thought, reflection, prayer, rite—they all aim at this existential consummation and finally, by the time a person dies, are absorbed into it.

Could we not deduce from this that we now live in a time when we ought to be led very intensely to this existential consummation? The twentieth century is the century of boundless mass sacrifices and holocausts that silence any attempt at interpretation, justification, pious dictum, or rite. Today, the reality of Holy Saturday is so enormous, so unmediated, so relentless, that we can *only hold our tongues.* But when reality reaches for us so directly, should we wrack our brains about how to "save" and "preserve" all the practices, the ceremonies, the customs, leading to Holy Saturday? Might they not surreptitiously become pretexts and diversions, merely obscuring and obstructing our *view of naked reality?*

Our old breviary contained the edifying tale of the holy bishop Wilhelm, who, in the hours of his death, climbed out of bed, stripped off his pontifical garments, and lay down to die on the bare floor. At the last moment, but nevertheless in the nick of time, he had evidently realized that, at this point, all liturgy and all role-playing ceased and reality began.

*The Crisis of Religious Experience*

The posthumous writings of Romano Guardini include a letter of December 18, 1963, which talks of "the disappearance of religious experience":

> At a very early point, Rudolf Otto's religious psychology and religious philosophy on the one side, and Kierkegaard's theology, on the other side, drew my attention to the essential difference between religious experience and faith, between the numinous character of the reality of the world and of life and the revelation. It became clear to me that the experiences, acts, insights, shapes, etc., that form the first group are part of human nature, while the second group is based on free grace. The elements in the first group become stronger, the further back one goes in history; they diminish as scientific, technological, life-organizing development advances. "The religious" is a psychological, cultural element that—as such—changes with history, and in such a way that it steadily diminishes, if I see it correctly . . .
>
> A closer investigation leads one to suspect that a great deal of what was called "religion" in a summary sense, nay the act of faith itself consisted to a great extent of "religious" elements. This brings up the problem of whether revelation and faith themselves are bound to diminish with that abatement of religious experiences and acts of life.
>
> . . . If this religious element is lost to the world, then does revelation pass with it? If religious experience becomes senseless, does this hold true for faith as well? . . .
>
> However, the greatest danger, the power most destructive to faith, resides, so it seems to me, not in difficulties, objections, etc., that can be indicated, but rather in the spiritual emptying which takes place as the immediately religious keeps growing weaker. This

makes faith, religious acts, masses, sacraments, etc., arduous. One then has the impression that they are fundamentally superfluous, that we can get along without them. . . . The atheism spreading through the world seems to have its concrete basis here . . .

What does all this mean for Christian knowledge and Christian life, for instruction and education?

The goal cannot be to ignore them or to artificially enliven this waning religious experience by employing suggestive or pedagogical methods. Instead, the question must be posed more clearly: What does genuine faith in the revelation look like in a person or in an era in which this waning of the "religious" has become dominant? Does genuine faith belong to a specific period of historical development, or is it possible, in fact obligatory, in every period? If so, must we then assume that there is a historically determined situation of, psychologically speaking, "naked" faith, faith without religious experience—as appears to be borne out by the life stories of great Christian personalities, as well as experiences that every believer has at certain times in his life, above all in old age, experiences in which the act of faith is performed merely as an "achievement," as loyalty, as a realism that is not supported by anything emotional? (*Theologische Briefe an einen Freund,* Paderborn, 1977).

## The Crisis of a Specific Form of Monastic Life

During the nineteenth and the first half of the twentieth century, the monasteries, especially those of the Benedictine family, made a name for themselves as places of liturgical and—in Guardini's sense—religious culture. Thus, it comes as no surprise that today they are still widely expected to be solid bastions of a vanishing religious awareness, places where cult and ritual and a sacral atmosphere remain perceptibly alive.

The early monks, above all the hermits, lived in meager forms: cult, rite, sacraments, and so on, played a very subordinate role with them. When Abba Anthony, for instance, locked himself up for twenty years of solitude in an abandoned desert citadel, he obviously had to do without mass all that time, since he was not a priest. Characteristically, one of the didactic tales of the desert fathers tells of how the devil sought to tempt and trap a hermit who had been living in the desert for many years. The devil said to him: "You gain nothing from sitting here in your cell, because you never receive the body and the blood of Christ. I fear that you are becoming alienated from him because you are growing so remote from this mystery" (Apophthegma 1142 in *Weisung der Väter*, edited by B. Miller, Freiburg, 1965, p. 392).

In reality, life in isolation did not have to spell estrangement from the sacrament of the eucharist. On the contrary, it could be an existential involvement in this sacrament, a consequence of the sacrament. In the twelfth century, the Cistercian William of St. Thierry, who was inspired by the spirituality of the desert fathers, wrote along those lines: "Only few men [namely priests] are granted the privilege of celebrating the mystery [of the mass] at a specific time and in a specific place. However, it is possible for all men to perform and to get involved in the essential aspect of this sacrament or mystery [*rem* sacramenti vel mysterii] in any time and in any place" (Migne PL 184, 357B).

A radical denudation in solitude, such as the early monks experienced, has come down to us—granted, in totally different external conditions, but not so very different in quality. Could this not offer a possibility for a highly existential communion and participation in Christ's denudation in his suffering and dying?

*"Share Christ's Shame Outside the Camp"*

Could it not be that we are being asked, in a new, intense, and highly existential fashion, to hear and to obey that *Ite, missa est* which has been sung at the end of countless solemn services in rich, splendid melodies—to hear and to obey it not just in its aesthetic harmony, but also in its ultimate seriousness: go forth from the space of religious experience and have the mass that you have celebrated come true in your lives! Know it and affirm it as a calling and a positive value when God places you in the "situation of, psychologically speaking, 'naked' faith, faith without religious experience"! Forget about "artificially enlivening this waning religious experience by employing suggestive or pedagogical methods." Instead, go forth with Christ "outside the camp" of religious culture "bearing abuse for him" (Heb. 13:13): his temptation, his fear, his night on the mountain, outside in Gethsemane, on the cross, in the tomb!

This would not be a burden, but rather a chance to enter Christ's fate and be close to him.

This does not, of course, imply that we should now leave behind all liturgy, all cultic forms, and all the culture of ecclesiastical chant. In the mass, we continue to celebrate realities that surpass our comprehension and are meant to, indeed can, impart a vision of what we wish to enter and be completed in. After all, there are further aspects and meanings that justify the celebration of mass, even necessitate it. In the mass, the *Church* becomes visible as the community of the Lord and comes to itself. It keeps experiencing anew, in word and sacrament, the interpretation and explanation and dedication of its own destiny; it keeps receiving anew its calling and, symbolically and really—especially in the celebration of the eucharist—it is received into Christ's sacrificial surrender to the Father, i.e., raised to a sphere and a relationship that no amount of human struggle and sacrifice, however intense, could possibly achieve alone. The sacramental and the existential consummation of man's surrender to God are geared to each other, interpreting and complementing one another. The sacrament provides the deepest, ultimate perspective and establishes concrete contact with God; and the existential consummation gives the seen and seized man his extreme consequence, earnestness, and definitiveness.

Thus, the goal is to set one's sights on the possibility of evaluating the condition Guardini describes, namely that, for us moderns, "the religious acts are arduous," less negatively and passively. Rather, we have to grasp and affirm it as a specific form of our calling to the Imitation of Christ. Precisely at a time when our "religious" experience is vanishing and dying out, this could be a sign that we are being led from the celebration to the materialization that we who are hungry, thirsty, and blind are not so far from the kingdom of God as we feared. In his Good Friday sermon, the curate in Georges Bernanos's *Dialogue des Carmélites* says:

> In times that are less somber, the tribute to His Majesty easily assumes the character of a simple ceremony, far too similar to the homages paid to the kings of this world. I am not saying that God rejects this sort of veneration, even though the spirit suffusing them derives more from the Old Covenant than the New Covenant. But at times, he does weary of such tributes—if you'll forgive the expression. The Savior lived among us and is still living among us as a poor man; time and again, he decides to make us as poor as himself, so that he may be received and honored by poor people, in the manner of poor people, in order to rediscover what he experienced so often on the streets

of Galilee: the hospitality of the wretched, their plain welcome

## *The Consequence: Sobriety, Lucidity, and Simplicity*

The coming and the nearness of God in utmost poverty will dawn upon us only when we truly and positively accept the situation of apparent nonexperience, this Holy Saturday on which the altars are cleared. We must not wander off secretly to more interesting and more satisfying activities that provide us with the proof and the certainty that our life *does* have meaning, that it can be satisfying, that there is a reason for our existence. For periods of spiritual bleakness and barrenness, the desert fathers consistently advise: "Stay where you are, endure at any price, keep on as before." This advice holds for our present situation, too—not in the sense that we are to immure and defend ourselves in old forms and rites, denying and disguising every crisis, but rather in the sense that we must live consciously in and with this crisis, understanding it as a chance to enter, factually and physically, into Christ's renunciation, thus forging ahead on this path to the reality of a new life. This would release us from the paralysis caused by our fear and worry about our present and future, a paralysis that is completely fruitless and ultimately hopeless, because it comes from secret lack of faith. We would then be liberated to a deep, new joy that is bestowed upon the person who unconditionally lets himself fall into God's abyss—a joy that can develop new, creative forces.

Why not simply accept the present reality as it is? Let us omit from our masses everything tinged with pomp, bombast, and claptrap. Let us plainly and simply listen together to the dry but nourishing Word of God, and let us try to obey it; let us receive the sacrament whose essence and truth are grasped by faith independently of any sensing and experiencing! From this sober and unassuming core (and only from here), we will then gradually find our way back to the proper, suitable, and honest forms in which the Word of God can be grasped, expressed, and communicated. If we do not come from here, then all our celebrating remains a skillfully concocted folklore, an entertainment, or a hard sell of the "commodity known as God."

Marie Luise Kaschnitz, in her *Tutzing Cycle,* writes:

*You act rough with the people*
*Who still know you in the old way.*
*You let their hearts go bleak at your altars,*
*You strike them blind in your lovely valleys.*
*If they try to praise you*
*You wash the body up at their feet.*
*If they start to talk about your love*
*You reverse the speech in their mouths,*
*You make them howl like dogs in the night.*
*You may not want people to talk about you.*
*You used to feed on flesh and blood,*
*Feed on praise. Feed on the singing*
*Of wheels. But now you feed on silence.*
*You gather our blind eyes*
*To form the lunar lake of oblivion.*
*You prefer our paralyzed tongues*
*To the dancing wheels of your pentecostal miracle.*
*You would dwell more securely in the love shade*
*Of the desperate forehead than in the house of God.*

("Tutzinger Gedichtkreis," in Kaschnitz,
*Neue Gedichte* [Düsseldorf: Claasen, 1957] p. 13.)

These lines spontaneously arouse in me not a fear and anxiety that God is vanishing from us, but a feeling of great sobriety, lucidity, and simplicity. I am freed from the obligation of complicated words and rituals and customs; I am no longer dependent on all the media and materials that we now employ to make God palatable; I no longer have to work through tons of printed paper, which one supposedly must read in order to be able to talk about God in a modern and authentic way and with a correct awareness of the problems. Here, everything becomes infinitely simple and fascinatingly direct. What "nourishes" God is my silence and the "love shade of the desperate forehead." I do not have to serve Him with knowledge, with experience, with feelings, with grand sacrifices, or with wordy prayers. I only have to be *here* as the poor, empty, helpless, questioning person that I have always been. What "democratization" of the approach to God emerges with this insight after all the problems of theologizing and hermeneuticizing, which make God seem attainable only by specialists!

## The Peace of the Person Who Has Died in Christ

Everything now depends on not refilling this emptiness with hastily and artificially sought meaning. We have to abide in this emptiness and, beyond any "finding out" or "experiencing" in "naked" faith, we have to grasp that this is the mystery of Holy Saturday: to go through an Imitation of Christ, to consummate existentially His "descent into hell," the hell of isolation, hollowness, nonexperience, and at the same time, the immersion in this peculiar peace after surrender, the peace lying over Holy Saturday and opening itself as an intrinsic, far more essential manner of experience the further one enters into it. This peace is anything but a graveyard peace of the irrevocably dead and isolated. On the contrary, here, in this place, communication is fundamentally possible with all human beings. As long as they still articulate or interpret their pain or as soon as they put their joy into words, they speak different languages—their concepts and images collide in space and create all kinds of misunderstandings. But here, in the emptiness, where they are silent, as absolute paupers—here they all meet and understand each other, no matter what their philosophy, their religion, their denomination, may be. This is the common point of departure and point of destination for their existence. This is where I find them all. And this is the place from which words in common may be sought and found.